HIDDEN
BUCKINGHAMSH
Jean Archer

HIDDEN
BUCKINGHAMSHIRE

Jean Archer

with illustrations by Pip Challenger

COUNTRYSIDE BOOKS
NEWBURY, BERKSHIRE

COUNTRYSIDE BOOKS
3 Catherine Road
Newbury, Berkshire

www.countrysidebooks.co.uk

ISBN 1 85306 045 3

Front cover photograph of Newport Pagnell
taken by John Bethell
and
back cover photograph of Penn Street church
taken by the author

Produced through MRM Associates Ltd, Reading
Typeset by Acorn Bookwork, Salisbury
Printed in England by J.W. Arrowsmith Ltd., Bristol

Introduction

➤ The shape of the County of Buckingham on a map resembles a lion rampant, and its great pageant of history runs like a glistening thread through the tapestry of centuries. Mostly this history has to do with the fight for liberty from the Lollards of John Wycliffe, to John Hampden and to William Penn and the Quakers at Jordans.

It is also a county of varying scenery; every difference a delight. There are the Chilterns with their rolling beech clad hills that run in gentle slopes down to where the River Thames forms the boundary in the south. And there is the escarpment that stands out tall and sharp against the glorious Vale of Aylesbury with splendid views over its rich pasture land, ancient manor houses and clusters of thatched white-walled cottages. To the east are the low-lying water meadows of the River Thame, brimming with bird life, and to the north an unhindered countryside of pleasant undulations, wide views and church-crowned hillocks, and the River Ouse winding away into the next county.

This is the scenery that has given inspiration to such writers as Milton, Cowper, Shelley, and Gray. It has housed Prime Ministers, not only for the odd weekend at Chequers, but Disraeli at Hughenden and Portland at Bulstrode.

It holds the story of the lace-makers, the thatchers, the builders and farm workers, the people of the villages and towns who still retain an immense pride in their county. An old saying of my childhood 'I be Bucks, I be, and proud an it' is still to be heard from the south to the north and, coming as I do from a family whose roots go back at least two centuries in this county, I grew up listening to this pride in the countless stories that were handed down for generations from places and villages, enhanced by tones of real affection in the telling. And as I travelled about Bucks engaged on research for this book, I became aware of the great fraternity of the Bucks native. The dialect is the password.

There are many excellent and first class books on the history and topography of Buckinghamshire, but I was glad of the opportunity to write on the theme presented to me – 'Hidden Buckinghamshire'. Here was my chance to move around the county and settle on a building, or a remote area, or any item or piece of history which could have been overlooked or stood in need of attention or expansion, or that dwelt in the shadows of better-known history. Indeed there is much to see: bridges, monuments, churches, ruins, earthworks etc – to the researcher or explorer enough material to last three or four lifetimes or even beyond.

Every place, village or town I have written about I have visited, and in this respect I am grateful to two friends, Meg Green and Pam Appleby, who have accompanied me at different times on my expeditions. They both nurse a great interest in the county as a whole and anything I might have missed, they noticed. I am also grateful to the staff of both Amersham Library and the Bucks Reference Library who put up with my constant entreaties for assistance or requests for copying.

Lastly, my thanks go to the people I deliberately contacted or met by chance on my travels – their interest, help and friendliness will not be forgotten.

Jean Archer

Bibliography

Adam, A. E.	*Beechwoods and Bayonets*
Bergamar, K.	*The Bucks Explorer*
Camp, J.	*Portrait of Buckinghamshire*
Cocks, A. H.	*The Church Bells of Buckinghamshire*
Cutforth, J.	*Marsh Gibbon Friendly Society*
Eland, G.	*The Chilterns and The Vale*
Gibbs, R.	*The Buckinghamshire Miscellany*
Gibbs, R.	*Worthies of Buckinghamshire*
Lipscombe	*History of County of Buckinghamshire*
Mee, A.	*Buckinghamshire*
Perrin, B.	*No fear or favour*
Pevsner, N.	*Buildings of England Series – Buckinghamshire*
Robinson, R. M.	*Penn County and The Chilterns*
Sheenan, J. J.	*The History and Topography of Buckinghamshire*
Shorter, C.	*Highways and Byways of Buckinghamshire*
Sparkes, I.	*Stage Coaches and Carriages*
Strickland, A.	*Life of Queen Elizabeth I*
Toulson, S.	*The Drovers*
Verney, M. M.	*Bucks Biographies*

Buckinghamshire Victoria County History
Buckinghamshire Archaeological Society Records
The 'Little Guides' to Buckinghamshire
Buckinghamshire & Berkshire Life Magazines

Addington

➤ Addington is well and truly hidden from the world. It is approached from a turning off the Winslow-Buckingham road down a single track, which feels like a private drive as it also leads to the gates of the manor house. Once there the road swerves to the right and comes to a full stop at the delightful little church standing with a handful of houses and the peaceful rectory in deep green shade. Directly ahead a footpath dwindles away into a cornfield and at the church gate stands a huge, spreading chestnut.

There are not many hamlets smaller than Addington. It certainly has not grown; if anything it has dwindled. In 1712 the population was recorded as 17 families and 80 inhabitants – today there are just 70 names on the Parish Electoral Roll.

Yet in this secluded little church, St Mary's, there once hung a rare treasure – a picture from the ancient Italian city of Orvietto, some 600 years old and depicting Christ before Pilate. Tragically, in the late 1970s it was stolen.

Today it is the windows that are the 'stars' of this church. They comprise the largest collection of Netherlandish glass in England. The roundels are 16th and early 17th century mounted on Victorian painted quarries. These windows mostly illustrate biblical scenes and are both delicate and exquisite, their soft colours creating a pleasant glow inside the church.

When Henry VIII was seeking a divorce from his first wife, Katherine of Aragon, the Pope refused to sanction it. This rather upset Henry so he then renounced the supremacy of the Pope over the English Church. He went so far as to decree that the very name of the Pope must be deleted from Church books. By 1576 he had ordered the destruction of all Catholic books and this put Thomas Andrews, the priest at Addington, in something of a dilemma. His books had cost a great deal of money out of his meagre living and, what's more, he was extremely fond of them. So he walled them up in the north wall of the chancel of the church. And there they

9

lay hidden for some 300 years. It was in 1857, when the church was rebuilt and refurbished, that the north wall was pulled down. Then the books came to light.

There were six of them, all of the 16th century, one a Henry VIII primer (prayerbook). A note on the flyleaf of this primer describes the finding of these books in 1857 and adds: 'Besides these books was found a small slate slab let into an oak panel with chamfered edges. It has five crosses and the initial T.A.'

Undoubtedly, these initials were those of Thomas Andrews. The note goes on:

'It is believed to be the only example of an ancient Super (portable) altar to be found in England and is probably about the date of the 14th century.'

It had been decreed in 1550 that these altars should no longer be used and no doubt clever Thomas Andrews, fearing for its preservation, decided to hide this in the wall together with his precious books. During restoration work in 1858–9, this slab was let into the main altar.

The Reverend Gerard K. Olivier was rector of this parish from 1924–30. He was the father of Sir Laurence Olivier, who spent some of his early life here and sang in the church choir.

Furthermore, Sir Malcolm Sergeant, the famous conductor, lived in a cottage here during the Second World War and from time to time played the church organ. What church could have had two more splendid performers!

Amersham

It is true that at the foot of Ruccles Field there is a signpost, and halfway down Station Road there is another, but in the centre of the old town of Amersham there are no directions whatsoever to the Martyrs Memorial, which stands at the top of the field overlooking the valley. Neither is there any indication of its whereabouts in the comparatively new town of Amersham on the Hill.

The shortest route to it is via the footpath in Station Road, following the narrow way between the houses. To reach it from the old town, walk past the 13th century St Mary's church, over the 'humptyback' bridge, and follow the little Misbourne to the signpost pointing diagonally across a field which rises steeply. There, on the summit, tucked away in a corner, is the obelisk, behind a small hedge yet looking proudly out over the Chiltern countryside. Emblazoned upon it is the story and names of some half dozen towns-people who, in 1521, in a shallow depression just one hundred yards further along the crest of the hill, were burned to death upon the instructions and in the presence of Bishop Langland. Also named are other Chiltern martyrs, Thomas Harding for one, who was burned in a dell at Botley.

It had all started many years before when the disciples of John Wycliffe, the man who criticised the established Church to more effect than most, walked the countryside barefoot, clad in russet gowns, carrying staffs and preaching religious reformation. They spoke in the market places and in the churchyards, and the people flocked to hear them. Neither did their words fall on barren ground. On the contrary, in 1414 many people from Buckinghamshire and in particular from the Chilterns, made the journey to St Giles' Field in London (now Soho), where there was a great gathering of Lollards, as those who followed Wycliffe were called. But Henry V got to hear of it and, fearing rebellion, dispersed them with his men at arms. Many were arrested and condemned to death. Among those who were dragged on hurdles through the streets and hanged together on a special mass gallows, were three men from Amersham – William Turnour, John Hazlewoode and William Yonge, together with John Fynch from Missenden.

Over the ensuing years many of the people in the Chiltern Hills met secretly in their own homes to talk and to read illegal books on religion. By the year 1506, the Bishop had decided it would be prudent to hold an inquisition in Amersham, which went on for some months and resulted in the burning of William Tylesworth. His friend, poor Thomas Chase was one of those forced to bear faggots as penance at the burning and, as if this was not enough, was taken to the prison of Little Ease (which entirely lived up to its name) at Wooburn where he was kept in chains and regularly beaten and starved, prior to his execution.

After the inquisition, and its subsequent punishments, things went quiet on the religious front. It is difficult to assess exactly when Lollardy began to merge with the general movement of Protestant reformation, but in 1521 the Bishop received the worst reports yet from the Amersham area and came to the conclusion that things were as bad as ever, if not worse. The town was considered to be an absolute hotbed of heresy.

Once more, the Bishop's chaplains descended for the usual inquisition and the people were gripped in an icy atmosphere of fear and suspicion. Betrayal was the order of the day and the inevitable outcome was the burnings that took place at the top of Ruccles Field. The spot had been carefully selected by the Bishop so that the fires could be plainly seen from the town below. All the people were expected to witness, take example and be warned.

Standing today on the crest of the hill, it is not difficult to imagine the procession 400 years ago winding its tortuous way to the top, the wailing of the relatives and the chanting of the priests, and then to look across the valley, at the last view those brave people saw before the first flames shot skywards.

It was always said afterwards that nothing could be grown on that place and certainly corn did not flourish there. In 1811 it was recorded that a labouring man named Belch was employed to dig up the soil to ascertain why the corn did not grow and it was found that an old chalk pit had been filled with large flints. Shortly afterwards, Belch died. It was considered to be a visitation of God and came as no great surprise to the people of Amersham.

Ashendon

 Who is the mysterious knight whose effigy reclines in a long, low recess in the chancel of St Mary's church at Ashendon?

There he lies in chain armour, his hand on his scabbard and his legs crossed since the 13th century, listening to the winds that buffet and howl against the walls of the little church, for Ashendon straddles a 500 ft high ridge overlooking the Aylesbury Plain and the church itself stands at the very summit. He is made of Purbeck marble, which appears soft and vulnerable, and has been whitewashed to blend in with the rest of the church. It is obvious that at some time over the centuries the poor chap has been knocked about a bit, his neck broken or his head knocked off, and whoever has tried to repair him did not have much of an idea of the proportions of human anatomy, as his neck is now much too long!

His crossed legs point to him being a Crusader and yet his armour would appear to be of a later fashion. His shirt descends to his knees. His left hand holds his scabbard which hangs from a broad belt, while his right hand grasps the hilt of his sword as if about to draw it. On his left arm is his shield and he is ready to do battle.

But who is or was he? There are those who say he was a member of the Cressy family, who were once lords of the manor. There are others who have said he could be Sir John Bucktot, who gave the manor of Little Pollicutt to Lincoln College, but the armour would surely not fit in with a man of the cloth. And then again some say, including the label in the church, that he was a member of the Stafford family. Whoever he was, someone has thoughtfully placed a calor gas fire close to him to ward off the cold of the church – and outside the countryside from whence he came affords the most heavenly views over the Aylesbury Plain with the blue Chilterns in the background. The roads to Ashendon are necessarily long and steep but it is well worth the trip to see this picturesque village with just a few cottages, farmhouses and a pub down a winding lane.

But step into the pretty well-kept church, as did the writer, when preparations are underway for the harvest festival. It is empty, the ladies creating the decorations have gone home for lunch, leaving startling cascades of floral arrangements and flowers in buckets ready for use on their return. The font is crowned with dahlias, trailing cotoneaster and bronze chrysanths blending in surprisingly well with carrots and tomatoes.

In the north wall of the church there is a blocked up 12th century doorway which once led through to a chapel. Old masonry, discovered later, is piled artistically here and strewn tastefully amongst it are marrows, carrots, cucumbers, potatoes and onions. The produce of the rich earth outside brought into this stumpy, sturdy little windswept church as it has been year after year for as many centuries as that mysterious knight has lain in his recess.

Aston Abbots

This is a small village that sits on a hill off the beaten track between Aylesbury and Leighton Buzzard and, believe it or not, has a link with the North Magnetic Pole! The name is derived from the abbey, which was used as a country retreat by the Abbots of St Albans in the Middle Ages.

The Royal Oak, a well-timbered building with thatched roof, is outstanding at the entrance to the village. Built in the 18th century, it was registered and licensed at that time as an ale house. In the fireplace of the public bar can be seen the interesting old spit, consisting of a bar with two bell-like sections, which, when wound up and down, rotated the meat over the fire. Some fine houses and thatched cottages line the road leading to the green, which is divided into islands. The church of St James was entirely rebuilt in the 19th century, with the exception of the tower which is 15th century and has a noticeable stair projection.

But, you may well ask, what possible connection could this small, peaceful place have with the North Magnetic Pole? The answer is Sir James Clark Ross (1800–1862), one of the most successful early polar explorers, who discovered this North Pole. He lived in the abbey, now called Aston House.

The story of Sir James runs like an adventure story from a Boys' Own Magazine. To start with he was said to be the most handsome man in the British Navy, which he entered at the tender age of twelve as a midshipman aboard the *Isabella* under the command of his uncle, Sir John Ross. Almost immediately, they set out on an expedition to find the North West Passage, but were misled into mistaking clouds for mountain barriers. Sir James made three further voyages before he and a Captain Parry made an attempt to reach the North Pole from the northern shores of Spitzbergen, travelling with sledge boats over the ice. Other expeditions followed and by 1830 he had discovered King William Land.

It was the following year that he finally planted the British flag on the North Magnetic Pole, after he and his party had suffered great privations.

'Sir James Clark Ross, the first whose sole
Stood on the North Magnetic Pole.'

So ran the popular rhyme of the time, but Sir James did not rest on his laurels. In 1836 he crossed the Atlantic to relieve frozen whalers trapped in Baffin Bay. Then, sailing in the ships *Erebus* and *Terror*, he charted about one thousand miles of coastland and made a desperate effort to plant the Union Jack on the South Pole, but was unsuccessful and cruised instead into what is now called the Ross Sea. Passing Ross Island and the Great (Ross) Ice Barrier, he came across a volcano some 12,000 ft high, which he named Mount Erebus, after his ship.

Some ten years later, another great arctic explorer, Sir John Franklin, set out for the North West Passage in Ross's old ships, the *Erebus* and *Terror*, but, near King William Island, they became trapped in the ice. The crews abandoned their ships and set out along the arctic shore to find the mainland. They succumbed to starvation and scurvy and, sadly, none survived.

It was Sir James Clark Ross who led the first expedition in search of them, to no avail, and he was forced to return home. He died at his house at Aston Abbots in 1862. There is a stained glass window to his memory in the church.

A century later, in 1972, he and other explorers were

St. Michael's Church, Aston Sandford

commemorated in a special set of stamps issued by the Post Office.

Now, this great man, who travelled so many miles amid tumultuous seas and treacherous ice-fields, rests peacefully in the little churchyard of the quiet village that was his home from the sea.

Aston Sandford

It was in the year 1801 that the Reverend Thomas Scott first walked into the very small village of Aston Sandford to take up residence there as rector. He was already a theologian and writer of national distinction and, largely due to his brilliant six volume *Commentary on the Bible*, which was heralded as 'the greatest theological performance of the age and country', he was known as 'the Commentator'.

He was born in 1747, the son of a Lincolnshire farmer, and received only seven years' schooling, which by no means satisfied his insatiable thirst for learning. His father, a harsh man, was insistent that his son should work on the farm, performing the dirtiest work of a grazier, despite the fact that his health suffered due to exposure to all weathers. But the young Thomas never gave up hope of one day getting away from the farm. He read whatever and wherever he could, sitting with the beasts in the fields, along the stream's bank or huddling under hedges. He made a desperate attempt to become a candidate for ordination, but lacking the necessary parental consent and testimonials, he was sent back to the fields and an angry father. Still he persisted with his studies and in 1772 he was at last ordained and became a priest the following year.

He was appointed to the curacies of Stoke Goldington and Weston Underwood in Buckinghamshire and in 1781 succeeded John Newton as curate at Olney. Here he met and lived next door to William Cowper, the poet. The two men found much in common, particularly literature. In fact, Cowper revised one of Scott's books, which was a narrative of his own religious development, entitled *The Force of Truth*.

While his sons were growing up, Scott moved to London where he was made chaplain to the Lock Hospital and became a popular lecturer. It was at this time that he wrote his great *Commentary* which was incredibly successful and sold in large numbers, not only in this country but also in America. Just to fill in the time he learned Hebrew and brushed up his knowledge of Oriental literature.

Standing as it does in quiet water meadows, he must have found Aston Sandford ideal for writing. It obtained its second name from the family of Sandford who possessed the manor at the end of the 12th century. The tiny church of St Michael, extensively rebuilt and restored in 1877, has a weather-boarded bell tower. Around it are clustered just a few houses, including the rectory. This idyllic spot can have hardly changed at all since Scott's day, and one has only to stand in the churchyard to know some of the peace that he fully appreciated here.

The manor house is said to be one of the few domestic buildings designed by his grandson, Sir Gilbert Scott, the Victorian architect, who, in his *Recollections*, described one of his childhood visits to Aston Sandford and hands down a marvellous description of 'the Commentator':

'My grandfather was a thin tottering old man; very grave and dignified. He wore knee breeches with silver buckles, black silk stockings and a shovel hat. He had a black velvet cap except at church, when he donned a venerable wig. The barber who made it was a pious man, who himself put two sons into the Church. He walked over from Risborough every Sunday to hear my grandfather preach and a place was always kept for him at the dinner table. Family prayers at the rectory were formidable to a child, they lasted a full hour, several persons from the village attending them'.

Gilbert Scott then went on to describe some of his grandfather's servants:

'Old Betty, the cook; Lizzie, the waiting maid; and old Betty Moulder, an infirm inmate, taken in on account of her excellence and helplessness, were all patterns of goodness and even poor John Brangwin, the serving man, partook of the atmosphere at the rectory.'

'The Commentator' died in 1821 and the little church he loved was counted too small to hold the crowds that wished to attend his funeral. So it was held in the church at Haddenham and the service was taken by Daniel Wilson, later the Bishop of Calcutta.

He is buried at Aston Sandford and Sir John Betjeman in more recent years wrote of the rectory there: 'It is nice to be writing to the very house where Thomas Scott lived.'

Astwood

◀━ Up here in the most easterly part of the county close to the Bedfordshire border, the countryside is wide and sweeping and the views largely unhindered. Therefore, it is surprising to learn that the pretty church of St Peter in the village of Astwood suffered bomb damage during the Second World War. The church stands on the A422 road to Bedford, together with the inn and a few houses.

The old manor house of Astwoodbury was considered by Browne Willis, county historian, to be one of the finest houses in Buckinghamshire. The manor had belonged to the Cranmer family, but for some reason, the house was demolished in 1799. All that remains today of its former splendour is the octagonal dovehouse that stands on the hill up the Turvey road.

Up until the late 18th century, a dovehouse was a very necessary item. The birds it housed supplied plenty of meat and eggs when it was difficult to obtain fresh meat during the winter months. By law only the lord of the manor was entitled to have a dovehouse and his tenant farmers were often driven to madness to think that the birds from it grew fat on their cornfields.

In 1650 there were said to be over 26,000 dovecotes in England and that number certainly exceeded those in other countries. In fact, Fynnes Morrison, shortly after the death of Queen Elizabeth I, wrote of England that 'No kingdom in all the world hath so many dovehouses.'

The dovehouse at Astwood was said to have over 300 nesting places and dates from the late 17th or early 18th century. It is of three storeys and is now most attractively converted into a cottage with part of the old moat at the side. It is a pretty dwelling with neat front door and garden and a magnificent Great Dane at the gate!

Aylesbury

➤ Look hard at the top of the Market Square for the magnificent King's Head Inn, owned by The National Trust since 1928 when it was handed over by the Rothschild family. Tucked behind buildings of a later date, partially obscured by progress, it is one of the most interesting buildings in the town. Enter through the little alley that opens onto the facade of the inn, with coach arch and courtyard beyond. The large leaded, mullioned window on the left of the arch will immediately take the eye. It still has some of the original heraldic glass bearing the arms of Henry VI and Margaret of Anjou, said to commemorate their marriage in 1445. Also illustrated, among others, are the arms of Prince Edward who was killed at the battle of Tewkesbury. Three shields from it are in the British Museum and two in Westminster Abbey. This splendid window is in the bar, which was at one time the hall.

The earliest reference to the inn is in 1386 and it is thought that at one time it was the guest house to a monastery. Henry VIII was a constant visitor here when he was pursuing Anne Boleyn. She was known as the 'Fair Maid of Aylesbury' and her father, the Earl of Wiltshire, was lord of the manor. When the monasteries were dissolved, Henry was quick to seize the inn for the Crown and he subsequently gave it to Anne's father.

In common with other tradesmen in the town, the King's Head issued its own coinage or tokens, some of which can be seen in the County Museum around the corner.

Oliver Cromwell, with an eye to his own comfort, made the King's Head his headquarters when his troops occupied Aylesbury and it was here that he received the delegates sent by Parliament to congratulate him on his victory at Worcester. The chair in which he sat is now in the dining room.

A piece of the original inn walls, wattle and daub, has been exposed and is exhibited under glass in the spacious comfortable bar. This room is a small museum adorned with stags' heads and old pictures, historic belts and pouches, a mantrap, pistols and muskets of the Civil War period and an enormous clock of the mid 18th century by Neil Campbell of Aylesbury. The inn also has a priest's hole and a spy hole.

The weather was cold this particular April, and sitting on settles in the lofty ceilinged bar, light glowing through the coloured glass of the huge window, three elderly pensioners enjoyed the blazing log fire piled high in front of them. Their Buckinghamshire dialect was slow and measured with significant pauses, which is just how it should be, around them centuries of their county's history.

A small room at the side of the bar, seemingly a favourite place for the male customers to congregate, was at one time called 'The Glue Pot', no doubt harking back to Aylesbury's printing history, but sensitively the name has been abandoned due to present day associations with solvent abuse.

Beaconsfield

◄ The stone is certainly not hidden. It is there for all to see, yet no-one seems to notice it. It stands at the side of the Oxford Road, near Holtspur, in full view of the busy traffic that goes rushing by.

The boundary and tithing stone has stood there since 1827, recording an important local victory. Inscribed upon it are the words:

'3rd May 1827
Boundary stone of the Manor and Parish of Beaconsfield
The custom of tithing corn in this Parish is (and has been so immemorially) by the TENTH COCK and the ELEVENTH SHOCK.'

The payment of tithe to the Church, one tenth of the increase of all forms of produce, was very often levied from the farmers in kind, ie the tenth piglet, the tenth lamb, the tenth cock of hay, and so on, and had been a source of bitterness and friction from as far back as Anglo-Saxon times:

'We've cheated the parson, we'll cheat him again,
For why should the vicar have one in ten?'

Resentment was no less at Beaconsfield around the year 1823 when a local man, John Rolfe, informed the rector of the town, The Reverend John Gould, that he and others felt in all fairness that, whilst the tenth cock of hay might be grudgingly accepted as payment to the Church, he felt most strongly that payment should only be given of the eleventh shock of corn. The reason Mr Rolfe gave the rector for this was that, in the interest of drying, it was imperative that the corn be stacked into shocks and as this incurred extra labour, naturally the value of the shocks had increased by the time they were collected for the rector and, therefore, the payment agreed upon should not be 'one in ten' but 'one in eleven'.

Needless to say, the rector did not agree (to put it mildly) and went so far as to bring a law suit against Mr Rolfe for his temerity. He did so with absolute confidence in the result, but Mr Rolfe remained undeterred and stood his ground. The court found in favour of Mr Rolfe, who instantly became the hero of the town and surrounding area. Perhaps the victory went to his head a little as he seemed to derive great

The Boundary Stone at Beaconsfield

23

enjoyment from rubbing it in and, at his own expense, he caused the stone at the side of the road to be erected as a record for all to see for centuries to come.

Shortly afterwards, the Tithe Commutation Act of 1836 stopped payment in kind and tithes were commuted to a rent charge on land. By 1891, landowners were made responsible for the payment of tithes, the tenant farmer paying nothing other than that indirectly through his rent. Later Acts made sure that tithes were really a thing of the past.

Bierton

➤ It is still surprisingly easy to stand here in Gib Lane on the boundary of Bierton with Hulcott and imagine in an adjoining field the last gibbet in Buckinghamshire as it stood stark against the skyline. And it is still possible in the quiet of the countryside to imagine the interest and consternation it caused when the body of a gentleman by the name of Corbet hung and swung there for some 20 years.

It may have been that in the year 1773 the district suffered from an unusual number of rats and blocked-up chimneys, for Corbet, a rat-catcher and chimney sweep, was engaged to work in the area. During this time a young girl called Mary Holt died. One night Corbet, out for a walk with his dog, peered through the Holt cottage window and saw the bereaved father, Richard, kneeling before his daughter's coffin, praying. What came over Corbet is not known, but accompanied by his dog he forced an entry into the cottage (it is thought solely with intent to rob). Once inside he went one step further and murdered poor Richard Holt.

Now Corbet must have been quite as thick as a plank, because when he made his exit from the cottage he forgot all about his dog and shut him in with his victim! The body was discovered by the milkboy the next morning and all the constable had to do was follow the dog, who unintentionally betrayed his master by leading everyone straight to him. Corbet was arrested with some stolen property belonging to

Holt in his possession. He was tried, found guilty and condemned to death.

The post that formed the gibbet was 18 ft high and could be seen for some distance over the countryside. And it was said that the crowds that gathered to witness the execution on 23rd July 1773 were immense and the road absolutely impassable. After the hanging, the body was quickly encased in irons and strung up on the arm of the gibbet for all to see and take heed. And there it stayed – and stayed!

It was not long before there were numerous complaints from people saying they could not sit up in bed and glance out of their windows without seeing the gibbet and its gruesome parcel. Others said they could not open their windows because of the stench.

In 1774, a 'sporting character' passing through Bierton offered to pay someone to climb the gibbet and put black gloves on the hands of Corbet as he swung there and also to tie a black scarf over the face. A local shepherd considered this easy money at 2/6d and the job was done with alacrity.

By 1795 all that was left of Mr Corbet was his skull, which was still hanging there encased in irons that creaked and swayed in the wind. Some years after that, when the irons had worn away, it was taken down and kicked into a ditch. Part of the gibbet was used as a gatepost for some years until a Mr Watts bought the wood with a view to making some fancy articles and souvenirs.

Bledlow

Close to the Oxfordshire border, this village must be one of the most attractive in the county. Just above the low-lying meadows of the Thame Valley and beneath the high Bledlow Ridge, the whole area is a particularly lovely part of the Chilterns.

The long, steep road from the ridge down to the village seems unending, but never tedious, as views over miles of rolling countryside open up, revealing fields, meadows and woods stretching away into the distance with little knots of houses and the odd farm here and there.

Behind the village, up on Wain Hill, is the Bledlow Cross, cut into the turf, similar yet smaller in size to the one at Whiteleaf. Below this hill and Bledlow are the tiny hamlets of Pitch, Ford, Skittle and Holly Green, all at the end of tiny lanes.

In the village itself, church, manor house, farm, inn, cottages and mellow old brick walls seem to be all in the right place, providing the necessary ingredients and blend to make the perfect grouping. Holy Trinity church, made up of a variety of periods, from 1200 onwards, is approached via a path with high banks on either side where daffodils and primroses mingle in the spring. It is an interesting building with a Norman cup-shaped font, 13th century mural paint-ings, a candlestick with a mock flame and a lectern compris-ing a carved oak eagle shaped so that the head and wings support the bible. The bird turns almost completely round in an attempt to look the reader straight in the eye, which could prove disconcerting.

This flint and stone church, believe it or not, is perched precariously on the edge of a deep ravine where the tiny river Lyde bubbles and flows way down at the bottom. This stream is fed by scores of springs and rivulets, many of which issue from small apertures appearing way up and under the tall bank supporting the church. This gave rise to the saying by the widely reported Mother Shipton, self righteous old gossip, and one can imagine her saying it in an ominous country dialect:

'All those that live and do abide
Shall see the church fall into the Lyde'.

It may disappoint her to know, wherever she is, that no one has exactly been waiting with bated breath for this disaster to happen. Her answer to that would probably be 'There's still time'. However, the rhyme then goes on in a more cheerful tone:

'All those that live and do remain
Shall see the Church built up again.'

Was she referring to survivors?

This ravine, already remarkable for its beauty, has been made even more delightful by the clever idea of enhancing the aspect with water gardens. Just along the road from the church is a gate marked 'Lyde Gardens'. Neat, stepped gravel paths, flowers and shrubs on either side, lead down in maze-like fashion almost to the river where their task is taken over by boarding walkways along the ravine, complete with bridges and seats.

Dams and tubs provide waterfalls and clear pools of shimmering reflection. The 'musical box' sounds of those crystal springs and rivulets grow louder as they run down through kingcups to the banks of the Lyde. Joined by them, the little river gains confidence and, flowing away from this heavenly glen, makes its way along low ground by Towersey and into the river Thame.

Standing down at the very bottom looking way up to the church above, the cross on top even more remote, the whole is quite awe-inspiring.

Boveney

There is a marvellous view of Windsor Castle from Dorney Common where the cattle, seemingly with a sense of ownership, walk in leisurely fashion across the road that runs through the middle, expecting as of right that cars will slow down to allow their passage. They always get their way!

The turning to hidden Boveney is taken from this common down a lane that leads to nowhere else. In this secluded, peaceful hamlet which consists of only one or two houses, including the 17th century timber-framed Boveney Court, the hurrying, bustling world seems a long way off.

If you thought the hamlet hidden, the tiny church, dedicated to St Mary Magdalen, is even more so. It is approached down a footpath from the house, a field of ripening barley on one side and trees on the other. Suddenly there it is, so humble and small, built of rubble with a wooden bell turret, its Norman walls said to be over three feet thick.

Although the origins are obscure, it stands on a site that has been a place of worship since long before the Norman Conquest and is thought to have been a chapel of rest used by bargees and other rivermen when there was a busy wharf close by, which was used in the transporting of timber from Windsor Great Park.

Standing gazing at this building in its timeless setting, it is so quiet one would never know that just behind the trees, only a few feet away, flows the river Thames with boats of all shapes and sizes gliding by.

A walk along the river path presents an idyllic scene with boughs from a variety of trees bowing down to the water, with no-one save an eager mother duck and her family and a single swan for company plus the odd boat at mooring. This is surely one of the most heavenly yet least frequented places in the whole county.

Calverton

Mrs Grace Bennett, widow of Simon Bennett, lord of the manor, had not always been so stingy. Perhaps the death of her husband in 1682 had something to do with it. He had been a Roundhead during the Civil War, but had received a pardon at the Restoration of The Monarchy in 1660. From him she inherited 'a prodigious estate' and carried on living at the 15th century manor house, near the church, running the affairs of her farms and woods herself.

Or it may have been because she nursed an obsessive dislike for the rector, the Reverend Carpender. Mind you, he wasn't too keen on her, especially after she tried to defraud him of his tithes. There had been times when she had given quite generously to church charities, but suddenly she stopped, and there is an entry in the parish register for 1689 respecting a collection for poor Irish Protestants which reads 'Madam Benet with all her wealth gave nothing.' It was not long before she was being described as 'covetous, stingy and hard to the poor.'

The villagers, as was the custom, were allowed to enter the woods to gather fuel for their fires, but she soon put a stop to that, instructing her keepers that every person that was caught 'sticking' in her woods should be seized and well thrashed, as she averred her wood should burn only on her own fire and not on that of anyone else. Even then she mistrusted her keepers and was plagued by the thought that her commands were not being carried out. She decided to test them personally and, disguising herself as a poor villager, her head covered by a shawl, she cautiously entered one of her woods. A wily keeper spotted and recognised her immediately in spite of her disguise. But he affected not to, and despite her cries that she was Mrs Bennett, he gave her a sound thrashing, which he must have thoroughly enjoyed.

The matter of her refusal to pay the rector his tithes ended in a lawsuit. But before the matter could be resolved, a most tragic event took place. It was well known in the area that the lady kept a great deal of money in the manor house, which sorely tempted a certain butcher from Stony Stratford, said to be her cousin, and on the night of the Stony Stratford Horse and Hiring Fair, he broke into the house and murdered her in the servants' hall, then made his escape over the wall at the rear. Nevertheless, he was caught, and was tried in an upstairs room at the Cross Keys, which once stood in the High Street at Stony Stratford. He was found guilty, executed and hung from the gibbet in Gib Lane at Calverton. This lane ran parallel with the wall which surrounded the orchard and warren of the old manor house and was formerly a part of the old packhorse road. It is said that the site of the gibbet is marked by a carving in a stone on this wall which depicts the outline of two gibbets and the date 1693. There is a discrepancy here, if indeed this date refers to the execution of the murderer of Mrs Bennett, as this did not take place until 1694.

Nevertheless, the carving is still there to this day and to

see it drive up the road to the church, turning right and skirting the churchyard. Turn left and walk about 50 yds to a farmyard gate on the left. Ignoring the usual farmyard odours, progress along the wall for some 30 yds. Some 3 ft from the ground you will see the stone, its carvings still discernible, though faint. One school of thought says that this is the spot where the murderer escaped over the wall.

Keep a sharp eye out, for the place is said to be haunted by the ghost of Mrs Grace Bennett!

Chalfont St Giles

It is possible to stand in the middle of the Chiltern countryside and be reminded of the swaying palms and golden shores of the South Seas, for what name conjures these more to mind than that of Captain James Cook (1728–1779), explorer, discoverer and hydrographer.

It was in the grounds of The Vache, once the manor house of Chalfont St Giles, that Admiral Sir Hugh Palliser (1723–1796) erected a memorial to his friend Cook after he had been killed by angry natives in the far away islands of Hawaii.

Both Yorkshiremen, their naval careers had run more or less parallel, for it was Palliser who had seen the potential of Able Seaman Cook when he was under his command on the *Eagle*, a ship of 60 guns. He was so impressed that he arranged for Cook to be appointed Master of the *Mercury*, in which Cook sailed for North America to survey and chart the course of the St Lawrence river. Although it was the first time he had undertaken such a task, he produced such an exact chart that his superiors were greatly impressed with his brilliant efficiency and thoroughness.

When Palliser was appointed Governor of Newfoundland, he sent for Cook and appointed him 'marine surveyor of the coast of Newfoundland and Labrador', and it was due to Palliser that Cook received a commission and was put in charge of the *Endeavour*. Palliser also backed Cook on his three great voyages of discovery which led to the exploration and charting of the coasts of Australia and New Zealand.

It can be wondered how Cook's career would have progressed without Palliser. The two men were also great friends – Palliser was godfather to Cook's eldest son who was named after him – and it was Palliser who worried about Cook on that last fateful voyage and grieved when the news of his death reached England. Out of his great respect, he erected the memorial in his park. It is a tower of brick and flint, standing high on a mound, surrounded by a moat. A wooden staircase gives access to a flat roof with a marvellous view of the house and park. Beneath this, on the floor below, a model of the globe stands on a pedestal with a eulogy of great praise 'To the memory of Captain James Cook, the ablest and most renowned navigator this or any other country has produced.'

Sir Hugh, though rendering his country great service in a most courageous manner (he had commanded the British Fleet at the battle of Quebec) was not so popular as his friend, and he became notorious rather on account of a court martial he had demanded upon Admiral Keppel. Apparently, during a naval expedition in 1778 against the French Fleet, Palliser's ship had drifted away from that of Keppel and the others, and although signalled repeatedly to come back into formation, he did not do so until nightfall.

The next morning the French ships were out of sight and the British returned to Plymouth, not a little disappointed. The newspapers blamed Palliser for the failure to engage the French and, although no charge had been brought against him by his colleagues, he demanded a court martial on Keppel, who was completely exonerated and acquitted. Sir Hugh came off by far the worst as the charges brought were pronounced 'malicious and illfounded.'

Publicity had roused the London mob against Palliser and they went so far as to gut his house in Pall Mall by fire. In York, the house of his sister was attacked and she was said to have gone mad with fright. He then made his second and perhaps greatest mistake of his life. He resigned all his appointments and demanded a court martial on himself! Once again it excited immense public interest with himself as the villain, and although the court recorded that his conduct had been spotless, they did feel that he should not have

shown such neglect for signals. The outcome was not unanimous and Palliser did not come out of it with honour. He asked for his appointments back. They were not forthcoming, and he was made a Governor of Greenwich Hospital.

He had purchased The Vache in 1777 and now he returned to his home like a wounded animal. He immediately sent word to the minister of the parish of Chalfont St Giles requesting him to have the church bells rung to signify his return. The minister refused saying that, as Sir Hugh had never set foot in his church, he did not deem it proper, adding significantly 'especially at this time.'

Sir Hugh then, through a servant, gave a guinea to each of the bell ringers if they would do as he asked. They decided to give him 'rough music', which was an old custom performed by villagers when they wanted to show disapproval and indignation against someone who had outraged propriety. After sunset, they assembled outside The Vache where they made an appalling din with warming pans, sheep bells, tin kettles, cow horns and other noisy instruments 'being such applause as they thought his detestable conduct deserved.'

It hurt, and poor Sir Hugh withdrew from the world, rarely leaving The Vache and nursing wounds he had received in the service of his country which were said to give him much pain and suffering. He died in 1796, a bad-tempered, irascible old man, leaving behind his historic house and his memorial to friendship.

Chalfont St Peter

◄ The Colony for Epileptics at Chalfont was erected in 1895, the first of its kind in England and at its entrance stands a curious obelisk which bears no relation whatsoever to the Colony. It is 60 ft high and made of flint rubble, which Pevsner tells us is highly unusual. It has an inscription to say that it was erected by one Sir Henry Gott in the year 1785 and repaired in 1789; what damage it had sustained in so short a . time is not known. It also gives the mileage to such places as Chesham, Denham, Uxbridge and London. All other nearby buildings are obviously of a much later date, including the Colony, so that at the time of erection it was far from any sign of human habitation. There could have been no crossroads to puzzle the odd traveller so that he stood in need of any direction. Therefore, it is not surprising that many stories float around the Chalfonts as to its original purpose.

It has been said that it was built to mark the spot of the killing of a stag by a hunting party which included George III himself, no less. There is another story that this King, whilst staying at Newlands, Sir Henry's nearby house, became lost alone in a thick fog. He had begun to despair when through the swirling mist there loomed a village yokel. The King asked where he was, to which came the answer 'Peters be over there and Giles be over yonder.'

'But what is the name of this place where we are standing?', asked the King in desperation.

'This baint no place at all,' replied the yokel.

'Then we shall jolly well make it a place' said the King and is said to have persuaded Sir Henry to have the obelisk erected forthwith as a direction finder.

The fact that George III often visited Gott at Newlands is not really surprising as Sir Henry appears to have been the son of the King's head gardener. By sheer luck, he inherited

Sir Henry Gott's Obelisk, Chalfont St. Peter

a large estate from two ladies who had lived in Battle and purchased Newlands after it had ended up in the hands of moneylenders. He set himself up as a country gentleman, rebuilding the house and gardens and immersing himself in hunting and such other country pursuits. Nevertheless, he justified himself adequately as a useful Justice of the Peace, Deputy Lieutenant of the County and, in 1774, Sheriff. It came as no great surprise when he was knighted.

Just to add to the mystery of Gott's obelisk, which survived being struck by lightning in 1964, it is believed to be the third on the site. The 15th century original was said to have been built of timber and served as a direction finder as seen from Windsor Castle, which would appear to require eyesight of considerable quality.

The simple, and more prosaic, reason for the existence of the present obelisk may well have been that Sir Henry wanted to point the way to any visitors to his house at Newlands, of which he was more than a little proud.

Chesham Bois

➤ It stands on the crown of a hill overlooking the valley of the Chess and, although now looked on as something of an extension of Amersham on the Hill, it still manages to retain its atmosphere of a separate village. It is easily missed by many travelling between the neighbouring towns of Amersham and Chesham, as most take the main route, the A355, and few travel the other quieter road through the middle of Chesham Bois with its common, small green with war memorial and handful of shops.

It is said to have derived its name from the Bois or Boyes family who were landowners in 1276 and not from the woods that surround it. The pretty church of St Leonard is in a fine position and is approached via a long drive. Although it was restored in 1884, there are still reminders of the original medieval building with some brasses of the Cheyne family, lords of the manor in the 16th century.

The rest of the village is mostly made up of large houses with spacious gardens, making it for many years an enviable place in which to live. However, in recent times, the pressure of the development that has been suffered by Amersham on the Hill has been felt from time to time and it is to be hoped that Chesham Bois can stand its ground in more ways than one.

The woods are extensive and fine, and stretch down to form a border and pleasant division between Amersham and Chesham. Thankfully they are managed by the Woodland Trust, but perhaps the really surprising thing is that the manor house of Chesham Bois is far removed from the village and stands in lovely grounds at the foot of the hill into Chesham and in fact is well within the bounds of that town. It was built in the last century, purely as a home for his family, by a gentleman of leisure by the name of John William Garrett-Pegg, who bought the lordship of the manor although there was no manor house standing at the time, the previous one having been burned to the ground. Local flints were carried by horse and cart to enhance the exterior which has a Gothic appearance. It is now a residential home for the elderly.

Many famous people have resided at pleasant Chesham Bois, not the least being former Prime Minister Ramsay MacDonald. He had a weekend cottage in Bois Lane from 1906 to 1915, primarily to enable him to indulge in one of his favourite pastimes – wandering in the Chilterns.

Louise Jopling-Rowe was another resident and an artist of no mean repute. From at least 1919 up into the 1930s she lived at Manor Barn in North Road. Born in 1843 she was a notable personality in the artistic world of London from 1870 onwards. She had studied in Paris when her first husband had served there as secretary to Baron Nathaniel Rothschild. On their return she exhibited many times at the Royal Academy and other galleries and later in Paris and Philadelphia. She was widowed, and then married Joseph Jopling, a watercolour artist. They purchased a house in Chelsea with a garden overlooking the river. In this beautiful setting they ran Studio Sunday Afternoons at which from time to time all artistic London met together. Their friends included Oscar Wilde, Arthur Sullivan, Henry Irving, George Meredith and the painters Whistler and Millais to name but a few. Millais painted her portrait which was regarded as one of his best. All the excitement, gossip and thrill of that now famous Bohemian set in which she moved she recorded in her book entitled *Twenty Years of My Life*. Widowed yet again, she married George Rowe and tacked that name on to Jopling.

In 1919 living at Manor Barn she founded the Chiltern Club of Arts, which she would be pleased to know flourishes to this day.

Chess Valley

The river Chess, not surprisingly, rises in Chesham and it runs for a mere eight miles, most of it through Buckinghamshire, before reaching the Colne just over the Hertfordshire border near Rickmansworth. It dallies in picturesque fashion in the alleys and corners of Chesham and hovers amid the ducks and watercress at the western end of the town before progressing down Waterside, where it begins a partnership with the B485, producing a most delightful drive out. Gradually leaving the straggling developments behind, it runs on through the Moor amid clustered reeds and ancient willows. Allow the road to take you on as in a dance with the stream running parallel on the right, until suddenly, as would a frivolous partner, it suddenly changes to the left.

Carry on now as the route, a sheer delight, opens up into one of the most charming valleys in the whole of the county. Through the trees that fringe the tiny road, tantalising glimpses across the stream of smooth hill pastures are revealed as the river meanders through water meadows and silver willows. On the right Ivy House Farm – on the left Bois Mill with gardens that go right down to the waters' edge and where the trout fishing is said to be at its best.

Without warning, on the hill on the left there appears the

most splendid sight – Latimer House standing high over-looking the valley is incredibly imposing and just in the right place. This was the seat of the Cavendish family who had owned the manor since 1615, and in 1863, just before Charles Compton Cavendish was made Lord Chesham, they built this present house on the site of an older residence where Charles I had slept as a prisoner and, a few years afterwards, his son, later Charles II, stayed before his flight to the Continent.

Looking around, it is not surprising that Sir Gilbert Scott, the notable Victorian architect, himself a Buckinghamshire man, called this spot 'a little paradise'.

But on, and follow the rippling, zig-zagging stream until you reach the signpost to the village of Latimer. Don't bother to resist it and drive just a little way up, arriving at the Neptune Falls where the road crosses the Chess. Clearly seen to the right is the footpath that runs close alongside the river. A matter of some 200 yards along this way is a most uncommon sight that will make the walker of any age or disposition stop dead in their tracks. Here at the side of the path is a grave or tomb built of brick with a flat stone slab on top which bears the inscription:

'Sacred to the memory of
Mr William Liberty of Chorleywood
Brickmaker
who was at his own desire buried
in a vault on this part of his estate
He died 21st April 1777 aged 53 years'

His wife followed him at a somewhat leisurely pace. She was also interred here:

'Alice Liberty – who died 19th May 1809 aged 82 years.'

There were those who said that Mr Liberty had fallen out with the church and so wished to be buried outside its churchyard – and remembering that the old church of Flaunden, which has now completely disappeared, was not too far away, this theory is feasible.

But it was certainly not unknown in those days to be buried on a pleasant piece of your own land. Mr Liberty may well have seen close by at Cokes Farm, Little Chalfont, the tomb of the Grimsdells where Farmer Richard Grimsdell had been interred in 1647, to be followed by members of his family up until 1739.

And then again at Great Missenden, some two miles from the parish church, on a hill overlooking the way to Wendover, was the huge Backhouse tomb, shaped like a pyramid, and some 11 ft square and 18 ft high. Captain Thomas Backhouse was interred there by his own wish in June 1800, on his own land standing upright and with his gun by his side. However, he had stood there for only seven years when one of his sons returned from abroad and removed the coffin of his father to the churchyard.

But the grave of Mr Liberty of Chorleywood is still there for all to see and, taking all in all, who could possibly blame him for wishing to be buried in his favourite orchard at this halcyon spot in the Chess Valley at the side of a lazy river.

Chetwode

Way back around the 12th century, this locality was terrorised by a ferocious wild boar of unusually massive proportions. This beast ravaged villages, even killing children, and plagued farmers until a hero by the name of Chetwode, a local landowner, took it upon his shoulders to rid the countryside of this scourge. He hunted the boar and, after a prolonged and particularly bloody battle, killed it, thus bringing peace and safety to his neighbours.

As may be guessed, he did not go entirely unrewarded. Apart from being feted as the local hero, he was granted the right of Rhyne Toll to the grateful area, extending to his heirs forever. This meant that, during the period commencing 30th October to 7th November in every year, Chetwode was entitled to levy a tax at the rate of two shillings per score upon all cattle and/or swine 'on the drift' or being driven through the townships or hamlets of Gawcott, Lenborough,

Preston cum Cowley, Hillesden, Tingewick, Barton and Chetwode. As will be realised, all tolls need collectors and in addition to one or two men stationed in various villages, boys of the area fulfilled a most important role.

The custom was that at 9 o'clock on the morning of 30th October, a horn was blown on Church Hill at Buckingham, and a voice boomed out 'This is Sir John Chetwode's Rhyne Toll'. This signified that the Toll had begun, whereupon beer and gingerbread were distributed to the boys of the village gathered there. When all had eaten and drunk their fill, the procession made its way to Tingewick where the same horn blowing, announcement and distribution of refreshments was made to the boys of that village. From thence to the Red Lion at Finmere some three miles hence where an identical procedure took place. The Toll was now in full force and the boys, each with a horn slung over his shoulder, set about looking for the cattle and swine. When they found the beasts, they blew on their horn, counted the number and demanded payment. All in all an enjoyable week was had by all and this custom only came to an end in 1875.

The story of the slaying of the boar may seem rather far-fetched and yet it was corroborated to some extent in the 19th century. It was during an enclosure of 1810 that an attempt was made to level a large mound surrounded by a ditch which from time immemorial had been called by the local people 'Boar's Pond'. This mound was situated within a mile of Chetwode Manor House and a certain tenant farmer hoped to bring the mound into cultivation. However, he received quite a shock when he unearthed the remains of a boar of tremendous size. It seemed obvious that the animal had lain full length on the ground, possibly where it had been killed, and earth thrown up on it from all sides, thus forming the mound and ditch. The bones were the subject of an exhibition at Buckingham in 1855, and the field is called Boar's Head Field to this day.

It should also be taken into consideration that a somewhat similar event is said to have taken place at Boarstall not too far away when a fellow by the name of Nigel performed the same service to the community by killing yet another boar of similar proportions. It would, therefore, appear safe to assume that this part of Bucks, near the Oxfordshire border, was once the terrain of boars possessed of rather nasty natures.

In the church, once the chancel of an Augustinian Priory, the Chetwode family box pew, tucked away from the sight and hearing of the main congregation, has a fire place in one corner which presumably was lit to ward off the cold.

There are some fine Early English windows in the building and Sir Gilbert Scott recorded how he sat entranced before some of the best early stained glass in the county.

There was some bright green damp amid the stones around the base of the font, and cowering away against the wall, desperately hoping that he would not be seen, was a small toad. All God's creatures!

Chilton

Here we have another mysterious knight, as at Ashendon, but this time he is not inside the church but outside, way up on the east wall of the nave near the roof, and only visible when standing against the wall of the churchyard. He stands in an upright position and he too has his legs crossed. He is clad in chain mail and a long, loose surcoat with his sword and shield at his side. He presents an even greater puzzle because apart from the question of his identity, he poses two more – what is he doing up there on the roof and, perhaps most important, how on earth did he get there?

He is said to date from 1280 and is thought to have been removed from the inside of the church and placed in this elevated position when the nave was heightened in the 16th century. Yet Lipscombe, the county historian, was of the opinion that he was moved to this extraordinary position when the tomb of a knight in the church was disturbed to make way for the erection of the tomb of Sir John Croke. His opinion was reinforced by the discovery in 1828 of a stone coffin which contained bones that may well have at one time made up the mysterious knight. Be that as it may, in his present position he is filled with dignity and gazes steadily out over the churchyard wall.

Chilton is well worth a visit for it is a wonderful example of a village of yesteryear with its picturesque cottages and wide views. On a warm day in June, the cottage doors stand open to let in the scent of honeysuckle and roses from gardens filled with blue delphiniums and foxgloves.

The church of St Mary stands on a rise and is approached up a slope from the cottages nearby. The building presents a most unusual aspect, not only because of the knight with the love of heights, but because it has no lofty tower as do most other churches, and it rather gives the impression at first sight of being an ancient residence rather than a church. It does have a short north tower with a higher stair turret, but as the ground falls away steeply at the west end, the erection of the usual western tower was thought to be impossible.

Inside is the cool of centuries and the story of the people of Chilton long gone. The Croke chapel houses the early 17th century, large and elaborate monument to Sir John Croke, Knight, and his wife, Elizabeth, who lie recumbent amid their eleven children. The light for the lectern was created from an hour glass stand of wrought iron which was made about 1650. There are not many of these stands now remaining in England.

Most touching is the original cross which was brought from the battlefield of Loos in the First World War where Lt Col Egerton of the Coldstream Guards was killed in action. It stands near the plaque to his brother, Louis Egerton of the Royal Bucks Hussars, who was also killed in that war.

Follow the knight's gaze out over the wall to Chilton House. Sir John Croke built the first house, which was in great jeopardy during the times of the Civil War when Prince Rupert feared that it may provide a garrison for the Parliamentarians 'which may annoy and incommode His Majesty's quarters', and he therefore gave orders to 'demolish, raze, and render it in such a condition that it may not anye wayes be useful to the Enemye.' This order was countermanded and the house remained in its old state until it was pulled down by the then owner, Judge Carter, who erected on the site the present mansion, said to be on the same lines as Buckingham Palace.

It is now a nursing home where residents enjoy the marvellous views over the chequered Buckinghamshire countryside.

Coleshill

Coleshill is a pretty, sought after village that stands on a hill overlooking the town of Amersham. It has a church, a pub, a common, a village hall, a windmill, some splendid houses and attractive cottages. It also has a remarkable tree called 'Waller's Oak', which is said to be 43 ft in girth.

Tradition has it that the poet, Edmund Waller (1606–87) sat in a hollow of this tree, overlooking the valley and woods towards Woodrow and composed some of his loveliest verse. He was born at Coleshill Manor House (Stock Place). His mother was a member of the Hampden family, which made him cousin to John Hampden and also distantly related to Oliver Cromwell. His father died when Edmund was very young, but he left his son an income of £3,500 a year which could provide for considerable comfort in those days. Mother became a force in his life and, it is said, arranged for him to become MP for Amersham at the tender age of 16. From the records it would seem his age was more like 21, but even so, this was surprisingly young. However, he was extremely eloquent in the House and possessed an outstanding command of the English language. He married the wealthy Ann Banks, which enhanced his fortune, but was a widower by the time he was 25 years old.

He fell passionately in love with Lady Dorothea Sidney, eldest daughter of the Earl of Leicester and sister to Algernon Sidney, another MP for Amersham. She would have none of him and married another, but his unrequited love brought forth some of his finest poetry:

'Go Lovely Rose
Tell her that wastes her time and me
That now she knows
When I resemble her to thee
How sweet and fair she seems to be.'

He perked up and married a lady by the name of Mary Breaux by whom he had 13 children.

By now, he and his mother had purchased Hall Barn at Beaconsfield and it seemed naturally to follow that, at the outbreak of the Civil War, he should stand with his cousins, Hampden and Cromwell, but in 1643 he became involved in a Royalist plot which, when uncovered, led to his imprisonment in the tower when he was forced to pay up £10,000 to save his life. His behaviour at this time was anything but gentlemanly. He betrayed others and pleaded cringingly for his life. He was exiled and lived mainly at Rouen for some years.

On his return he tried to ingratiate himself with Cromwell and wrote a panegyric poem about him. After the monarchy was restored in 1660, he wrote a similar poem, full of praise for Charles II, but the King was no fool and remarked that it was not nearly so good as the one he had written for Cromwell. Quick as a flash, Waller replied 'Sir, we poets never succeed so well in truth as in fiction.' Charles threw back his head and laughed, and Waller was restored to his former position.

Edmund Waller's politics were changeable to say the least, but it must be remembered that he was a sensitive poet living in troubled times. He was attractive, charming and witty.

Was it whilst sitting in that oak at Coleshill that he wrote the saucy poem *On a Girdle*?

'That which her slender waist confined
Shall now my joyful temples bind;
No monarch but would give his crown
His arms might do what this had done.'

Towards the end of his life he longed to return to Coleshill and tried to regain his birthplace, as in his own words 'A stag when he is hunted and near spent, always returns home.' But it was not to be, and he died at Hall Barn at the age of 81.

Colnbrook

If there was an inn where a traveller could be sure of the warmest of welcomes in the 17th century, it was at the Ostrich at Colnbrook. From the very first moment he arrived in the inn yard, he could not help but be favourably impressed by the quick service and efficiency of the ostler who

The Ostrich Inn at Colnbrook

45

rushed forward to take his horse for stabling and to carry his bags (carefully feeling the weight at the same time). Also by the friendly greeting of the exceptionally genial landlord, Mr Jarman. Why on earth should he notice a whispered conversation between the two, or indeed anything untoward in the call of the landlord to his spouse: 'Wife, there is a fat pig to be had, if you want one.' Nor any sinister implication in her reply 'Prithee put him in the sty till tomorrow.'

Shown up to the Blue Room, the best in the house, he would soon be refreshed and ready to descend to a dinner fit for a king, the landlord being particularly anxious that he should try some of his best wines. At this point, a delicious drowsiness usually came over him and bidding a 'Goodnight' to surely the most perfect landlord ever, he then made his way up the stairs to the most comfortable of beds, beautifully carved. He would have no reason to notice that its feet were nailed to the floor. Climbing at last between snow-white sheets, and sinking down into the soft mattress, he drifted into sleep – WHEN BANG – a trapdoor was sprung which opened the hinged bedstead and the sleeper slid head first through the floor to the kitchen below and into a cauldron of boiling brew that was awaiting him.

This was the normal routine of Mr Jarman and his wife that brought instant death to at least 13 travellers. Afterwards, with practised swiftness, the trapdoor was replaced, any valuables removed together with clothing and the body taken out and disposed of in the river Colne. The next morning anyone enquiring about the murdered guest would be told that he had risen and left before dawn. His horse would have his tail, mane and ears cropped and be hidden away for a certain length of time before he was let loose.

This unscrupulous couple at last came unstuck over the murder of a wealthy clothier by the name of Thomas Cole of Reading, sometimes thought to be the original Old King Cole of nursery rhyme fame. He had stayed at the Ostrich many times and slept in the death chamber but always seemed to have the most amazing luck. It seemed to the Jarmans that they just could not kill him. Just as they had him all lined up, something would happen to foil their plan.

On one occasion he was about to retire, when a messenger arrived from London and he had to leave hurriedly, and on another he asked for someone to stay by his bed all night as he felt ill. Yet another time he arrived with a fellow clothier, who shared the room with him. The Jarmans were grinding their teeth with frustration.

Eventually, old Cole's run of luck came to an end. He arrived at the Ostrich one evening incredibly tired, barely able to keep awake. The solicitous Jarmans pressed him to a quart of burnt sack, yet still he would not go to bed. He called for some musicians, did not think much of them, and dismissed them – and took another drink. The Jarmans had never had such a difficult customer and they hesitated at this point as to whether they should go through with it, but Cole had left a large bag of gold in their care, which Mrs Jarman found hard to resist. Finally Cole took himself off to bed.

Down in the kitchen with the boiling vat, Jarman was still hesitant, but his wife remained adamant. And so the usual operation took place and poor old Cole was foully murdered. But even then it seemed that in death he was still balking them. His horse escaped and ran straight for home. A manservant of Cole recognised it and went to the nearest Justice of the Peace. At the same time, it was discovered that Jarman had fled the inn, leaving his wife to be arrested. However, it was not long before he was captured at Windsor and the two of them confessed to many such murders before being being hanged at Tyburn.

Part of Colnbrook is in Buckinghamshire and part in Middlesex with the river Colne running in the middle. There was a time when it was a municipal borough and market town, but it lost its charter in the 17th century.

The rambling old timber-framed Ostrich is still there looking much the same with its archway and is proudly advertised as being the third oldest inn in Britain.

Due to the terrible state of the roads in the Middle Ages, mud-stained visitors for Windsor often alighted here to change into their official robes so as to arrive at the Castle in an immaculate condition.

Although the interior has been altered and improved, it

still retains the atmosphere of the popular coaching inn it became in the 18th and 19th centuries. And in the bar is a working model of the bed the Jarmans used for their victims, just to show how it was done!

Cuddington

Do not think for one moment that you have seen Cuddington when you follow the winding main road through from Dinton to Chearsley. It is well worth stopping to take a walk around this captivating village with its back lanes and two greens encircled by cottages of all shapes and sizes. The 12th century church was enlarged and altered no less than four times during the 13th century, which makes for interesting viewing. It was restored by Street in 1857. The handsome stone Tyringham House or Hall has the date 1609 over the doorway.

But it is those cottages of witchert that are so fascinating and attractive. Many of them are thatched and each has a character of its own. Witchert is a building material unique to Buckinghamshire. It is a white clay substance (its very name probably being a corruption of 'white earth') which is to be found only within the area of the villages of Haddenham (where it has been used most extensively), Cuddington and Lower or Nether Winchendon. At Cuddington it may be found in the gardens only three to four feet from the surface.

Mixed with a certain amount of water and chopped straw, it provides a sticky, clinging material which adheres to boots, tools, clothes and treads everywhere. The witchert builders are easily identifiable by the white crust that stolidly resists attempts at removal.

This 'gunge' is built up in layers of two feet at a time from the cottage foundations into walls some two to three feet thick. It is essential that every layer is completely dried out before the next is added. This very pliable building material is ideal for the production of curved walls, as seen particularly at Haddenham, and hardens with time. Therefore,

48

witchert cottages are both durable and strong and very difficult to demolish. In fact, quite recently one cottage in the area caught fire and was completely gutted, but those witchert walls stood as firm as ever. A cottage built of this material is exceptionally cosy, providing wonderful insulation, so that central heating rarely needs to be used.

Other villages where witchert cottages may be seen are Chearsley, Westlington, Dinton, Long Crendon, Ford, Bishopstone and Nether Winchendon, where some have been ochre-washed to show that they once belonged to the Bernard Estate. At Haddenham, witchert has been used on a very large scale in houses, cottages and barns, and in the winding lanes of witchert walls.

Inns too have been built of witchert and a former one may be seen at the Lower Green at Cuddington.

Denham

➤ It is not surprising that many famous people choose to live in the village of Denham hidden away between the Oxford Road and the Rickmansworth Road, as it is still surprisingly peaceful and picturesque with cottages, church and old houses of charm. Today there is no indication whatsoever of the tragedy that befell it in the 19th century and became national news.

Members of the congregation in Denham church that Sunday morning in May 1870 were puzzled. It was the first time that there was not at least one member of the Marshall family present at morning service. Emmanuel Marshall was the blacksmith in the village and lived with his wife and four daughters, plus his ageing mother, in a roomy cottage adjoining his smithy, which was some little distance from the Oxford Road. He was known as an upright, industrious man and an affectionate husband and father.

That weekend had been an exciting one in the Marshall cottage as Mrs Marshall's sister was to be married the coming Tuesday and was staying with them in order that they could all help in the wedding arrangements. One daughter was away staying with a friend.

There are several reports as to exactly how it came about that the bodies were discovered, but weight of evidence gives the time as the following Monday evening when the finished wedding dress was delivered to the cottage. Receiving no response to calls and knocks, the door was broken open and a most horrific sight revealed. In the hallway lay the body of Mrs Marshall hideously beaten about the face and head. At the bottom of the stairs were the bodies of the sister and two little girls aged eight and six. Further exploration revealed the body of the grandmother still sitting in a chair nursing the body of the youngest child, aged four. All had met the same ferocious end.

The police and other villagers arrived, but there was no sign of the blacksmith, and most people leaped to the conclusion that it was he, Mr Marshall, who, in a fit of madness, had killed his family in such a brutal manner. They searched everywhere for him to no avail, until they broke down the door to his smithy and there he lay in the same battered condition as the rest of his family. The doors of both house and smithy had been locked and the keys were missing. A search of the blacksmith's clothing also revealed no keys. The injuries to his head could not possibly have been self inflicted and, taking all in all, Denham had a mystery on its hands.

Then someone remembered that a notoriously bad character well known for his drunken idleness, a tramp by the name of John Jones, had been seen hanging about the place the previous Saturday evening and everyone was of the opinion that he could not possibly have been up to any good. The police, under the guidance of Superintendent Dunham, traced him first to Uxbridge and then to Reading. On arrest he tried to pull a loaded gun out of his pocket, but was overcome and brought before the magistrates of Slough. His bearing in the dock did nothing to recommend him and he was charged with the murders. Evidence was given that when apprehended he had in his possession the boots and watch of the murdered blacksmith and, as if that was not enough, he was also carrying the key to the cottage back at

Denham. Despite all this, Jones denied the murders and protested his innocence saying that two men had given him all these items as he passed the cottage. Additional evidence was also given that in fact he did have a grudge against Marshall in that the preceding January he had been sentenced to two months imprisonment upon the evidence of the blacksmith and at that time Jones had vowed a terrible vengeance. What could have been more damning than all that?

By now the murders were national news and it was with difficulty that the police prevented Jones from being torn to pieces on his way to Reading Station en route for Aylesbury. It was only due to a clever ruse and the laying on of a special train that he managed to reach Aylesbury Gaol in one piece.

At his trial he pleaded 'Not Guilty', but it only took two minutes retirement for the jury to unanimously return a verdict of 'Guilty'. The black cap was donned by the judge and the death sentence pronounced, whereupon the prisoner drew himself up, gave a military salute, and said 'Thank you, Sir.' This seems to have been the only polite remark he made throughout the entire time up to his execution. It was reported that he showed no sign of remorse whatsoever and maintained a callous indifference to his situation. Despite repeated attempts by the Reverend Bumberry, the prison chaplain, to bring him to penitence, he responded only with 'curses and foul expressions'. In fact, his only regret was that he had not shot the Police Superintendent. He showed no fear whatsoever, only aggression, and asked to see the hangman, Mr Calcraft, as soon as possible. He even asked if he could have his coffin as he said he would like to sleep in it the two nights before his execution. He had deserted his wife some twelve years before and he was rude and unfeeling when she visited him accompanied by his father. Furthermore, he flatly refused to attend Divine Service.

When the execution day dawned on Monday, 8th August 1870, there was a great deal of public interest. The condemned man had slept well and eaten a hearty breakfast, once again repeating his innocence.

He ran up the steps to the gallows two at a time, only to be made to come back and walk in an orderly manner, which would seem to be the last word in pedantry. He stood quietly over the drop whilst the hangman fastidiously adjusted the rope around his neck and pulled the cap over his face. Suddenly, Jones startled everyone by saying that he wished to speak. The cap was lifted from his mouth, and he said 'I am going to die for the murder of what's his name – I forget. I am innocent.'

He then obligingly placed his feet neatly together to be pinioned. The bolt was drawn and he was pitched into eternity.

Dinton

Dinton Castle or Folly must surely be the most eerie place for miles around. Although it stands on a mound only a few yards off the Aylesbury-Thame road, it is surrounded by tall trees, some of them the original firs, and jealously retains its seclusion.

It was built as a mock ruin by Sir John Vanhattem, then owner of Dinton Hall, in the year 1796, some say as an 'eye-catcher', some say to house and display his collection of fossils or as a summerhouse. Anything less like the latter cannot be imagined and anyway would entail a long walk from the Hall. Originally, the building consisted of a tower and two side towers. Today it is a hexagon with two remaining towers. It is built of stone with brick interior and, purely for ornamental reasons, huge ammonites are set in the stonework. The windows and archways are now just 'see-through' apertures and one of the towers is almost completely engulfed with ivy.

Whether Sir John knew that he was building his folly on the site of a Saxon burial ground is uncertain, but when the builders were digging the foundations, they found human remains, pottery and an old well. A century later it was decided to carry out further excavations which revealed a Saxon drinking glass and a bottle of the time of Edward III (c1350).

Dinton Folly

Believe it or not, this building was at one time home to an old couple by the name of Saunders, who had been servants at Dinton Hall, and who lived here as caretakers.

Now the 'ruin' itself has fallen into ruins, and would provide a suitable set for a horror film, perhaps one night when a rustling wind is sending clouds scudding across the sky and the full moon silhouettes the crumbling towers – or a bat swoops between the large archways and an owl hoots from an ivy-mantled crevice.

Whilst in such close proximity, it would be sadly remiss not to visit the village of Dinton itself, with its church, manor house and stocks on the village green.

The south doorway of the church of St Peter and St Paul has a remarkable Norman doorway and a tympanum with two dragons eating fruit of the Tree of Life. Dinton Hall was the home of Simon Mayne, friend of Oliver Cromwell and regicide, who expired in the Tower in 1661. His clerk, John Bigg, was the noted Dinton Hermit, who after the come-

53

uppance of his master, took himself off to a nearby cave and lived there in abject poverty until his death. There were those who strongly suspected that he was the executioner of King Charles I.

Dorney

◣ She was lovely, there was no doubt about it, and beautiful and captivating. She was only 15 years old when she first arrived in London and, left destitute by the death of her father, she was drably attired. But it did not take Barbara Villiers long to learn the fun and fashions of the city and such was her charm, in no time she had a queue of young men seeking her favours.

The moment Roger Palmer of Dorney Court saw her, he fell in love. After Eton and Cambridge, he had arrived in London on admission to the Inner Temple. His father, Sir James Palmer, loyal friend and supporter of the Stuart family and also a brilliant miniaturist, had purchased the manor of Dorney from the Garrard family around 1628, and he was not at all pleased when Roger told him of his plans to marry Barbara.

'If you marry that woman,' he said, 'I predict that you will be the most miserable man in the world.'

But Roger did marry her, and he was miserable, just as his father had predicted, for Barbara still continued a long standing affair with Lord Chesterfield and spent Restoration night literally in the King's arms.

Roger was made Earl of Castlemaine and Barbara, Lady Castlemaine, began her long run as chief mistress to Charles II which lasted until 1672. Roger eventually quit the country, serving firstly with a Venetian naval squadron and then with the English fleet. His half-brother, Philip, succeeded old Sir James and in 1665 his gardener named Rose grew the first pineapple in England. (Hence the inn named The Pineapple on the way into Dorney). This first luscious fruit was presented to King Charles.

Roger did eventually return to Dorney to help his brother out of financial difficulties. The property was conveyed to him, and the Palmers have been there ever since.

The little church of St James with its Tudor tower and 17th century red brick porch is not easy to find in a secluded backwater off the road to Dorney Reach. Inside this church a sense of mellow age pervades and the large encased family pew of the Palmers seems to bring to the mind's eye a picture of the congregation of long ago. The walls of the nave are Norman and the chancel arch is over 600 years old. At the west end is the most attractive feature of a musicians' gallery but it is in the north chapel that the essence of peace is to be found along with the Garrard monument. As was the fashion at that time in memorials, Sir William Garrard, who died early in the 17th century, and his wife, Elizabeth, are kneeling, facing one another, and below them their 15 offspring also kneel, five of them holding skulls to denote that they died in infancy.

Opposite the church, as if providing shelter, is Dorney Court, which is open to the public on certain days.

Dorton

➤ Deep in a dank, dark wood at Dorton there is a chalybeate spring which is all that is left to mark the days early in the 19th century when this small hamlet was well on the way to becoming a fashionable spa similar to Bath, Cheltenham and Harrogate. It was the brainchild of a gentleman by the name of Charles Spencer Ricketts, whose life would surely have seemed exciting enough without embarking on such an ambitious project.

His origins are unknown, but it is said that in 1795 he joined the Navy at the early age of seven and, in due course, served under Admiral Lord Nelson. He married a beautiful Buckinghamshire heiress, Elizabeth Aubrey, and retired from the Navy with the rank of Commander when he was only 27. He and Elizabeth had three sons and in 1825 his wife was bequeathed, among other things, the lovely Jacobean

Dorton House, which was surrounded by 400 acres of land. The will specified that the estate should pass to her sons.

Ricketts decided to make some money. He already had knowledge of a spring in the wood which the locals used for its healing properties. It supplied a pungent and revolting form of sulphur-smelling water similar to that available at Bath and an analysis showed that it was more potent than any other iron spring in the country and what's more, there was supposed to be only one spa in Germany of superior quality.

Mr Ricketts lost no time in promoting Dorton as the up and coming spa and it was given out that this water would cure a lengthy list of ailments from hysteria and indigestion to St Vitus' Dance, leprosy, dropsy and even blindness. An agency was opened in London for the sale of the water and back at Dorton, Ricketts, under the professional guidance of a Mr Hakewill, erected a Pump Room and baths taken from the design of the Tower of Winds at Athens. The building was entered through a magnificent portico supported by nine Corinthian columns and the ceiling, also supported by pillars, had a dome in the centre. There was a billiard room, reading rooms, ballrooms and a hotel. Pleasure gardens were laid out with fancy glades and flower bordered footpaths. Leaflets were printed with extraordinary stories of miraculous cures and Mr Ricketts was convinced that 'many a line of villas would speedily grace the spot.'

For a while Dorton Spa really did flourish – people seemed ready to actually leap into the waters. A warm chalybeate bath cost three shillings and sixpence whilst family and season tickets were available at reduced prices. Visitors kept the hotel going and before long the spa was receiving glowing reports in the press, such as 'this far-famed retreat which is expanding to boating on lakes' and 'this fashionable spa that has risen to eminence in the estimation of medical men.'

A tremendous firework display was held and musicians brought from London. Then came the news in 1836 that Princess Victoria herself proposed to pay Dorton Spa a visit, which, of course, would set it at the utmost pinnacle of success. But at the last moment she changed her mind and went to Leamington instead. Leamington soared to success whilst Dorton began to go downhill.

The hotel had never been adequate to provide for all and although it had been advertised that accommodation was available at nearby Brill, that village had only a couple of inns anyway. People did not only go to spas to take the waters, they also went to socialise, to meet old friends and to make new ones, so that the moment Dorton began to fade in the fashion stakes, its demise was inevitable.

A Grand Fete was put on in an effort to revitalise the spa, but little came of it and gradually all the grand classical buildings fell into ruin and today the searcher would be hard put to find one stone upon another.

Perhaps Mr Ricketts was cheered by the fact that he became the High Sheriff of Buckinghamshire. He must have been a man of some courage for, on the passing of the Reform Bill, the powerful Duke of Buckingham refused the people the use of the Market House at Aylesbury for a celebration. Ricketts, as High Sheriff, intervened and allowed them the use of the County Hall and also went so far as to give them a donation towards the cost. The Duke was not amused.

Drayton Parslow

➤ Most people are entranced by the name alone of this secluded little village that stands on a ridge overlooking the Ouzel valley, with a view of the Chilterns in the blue distance. It is not the only one to have the first name Drayton, there are many, and it has been suggested it may have something to do with drays or wagons – perhaps where they were made or repaired. The second name comes from the family of Passelaw, who from the time of Henry I, were lords of the manor for generations.

There is no trace today of the smithy and/or bell foundry that was once on land at the rear of the Three Horseshoes public house, although the ruins of the foundations could still be seen up until the end of the last century. It had once belonged to the famous Chandler family who formed a dynasty of bell founders and between them made Drayton Parslow the birthplace of many excellent bells during the 17th and 18th centuries.

It all began with old Anthony, who was the village blacksmith around the beginning of the 17th century, and it was his son, Richard, who was the first of the bell founders in the family. Just where he learned the art is not known for sure. It may have been at the nearby Buckingham Foundry, which came to an end only three years before Richard was definitely known to be founding. When he died in 1638, his son Anthony manfully took over the smithy at the tender age of 16. That business alone must have kept him busy for it was not until 1650 that he cast the treble for the village church at Simpson. This bell has been said to be one of the most strangely shaped bells to be seen in any church tower. It was this Anthony who made the clock that stands in the church at Whaddon. His son, Richard, also entered the family business and was dubbed 'Richard II', and it was not long before Richard III was founding bells!

During a sombre Commonwealth, no bells were known to come from this foundry, but with the Restoration came better times for all bell founders. There seemed hardly a bell in the county that did not bear the inscription 'Anthony' or 'Richard Chandler made me'. Those that did not have the Christian name of the founder but just 'Chandler made me' were considered to be a product of 'the Firm'.

1681 brought the first bell founded by George Chandler, and around that time the name of Thomas also appeared. The last bell bearing the name of Chandler was founded in 1726. Richard had died in April of that year and neither George nor Thomas carried on the business. For over a century this remarkable and skilled family supplied bells in a prolific fashion, not only in Buckinghamshire but also in at least five other counties.

Holy Trinity church stands on top of a hill, a handsome 18th century rectory just opposite. Inside the church is one of the finest fonts in the whole of Buckinghamshire. It is octagonal, of 14th century workmanship with sunken panels divided by buttresses, and has the most unusual feature of an embattled rim to the bowl.

But no-one should leave this church without looking at the alabaster panel in the wall behind the lectern. It is of the Crucifixion and in the 15th century was part of a set of six set into wooden altar retables. Not one complete set survived the Reformation, but the panel in the church at Drayton Parslow is considered by the appropriate department at the British Museum to be of above average quality. It is thought to have been carved around 1430 by the Nottingham School.

It may be that the inhabitants of Drayton Parslow have inherited a more than average flare for horticulture, for here in the church in 1630, when old Richard Chandler was busy in his smithy down the road, Archdeacon Sharrock, son of a 17th century rector, was baptised and it was he who wrote, among other works, *A History of the Propagation and Improvement of Vegetables*.

Emberton

◄── The Reverend Thomas Fry must have loved his wife very much for the memorial he left to her stands, complete with flagpole on top, in the middle of the village street. It is a clock tower said to have been erected in 1845/6 and is in the Early English style with lancets as bell openings, three on each side. The clock itself was presented by a Miss Hughes of Emberton together with the bell. It is an imposing and picturesque sight amid the old limestone houses and red brick cottages, interlaced with cobble and brick footpaths.

The Reverend Fry had been admitted to the living at Emberton in 1804 and served people and parish well for nearly 60 years. He was a man of uniform habits who drove regularly into Olney in a small cart pulled by two donkeys. When his wife, Margaret, died he hit on the idea of a clock tower to make sure that she was remembered, while at the same time providing the community with something worthwhile.

The village of Emberton is a neat village of size on rising ground in the Ouse Valley area astride the old Newport Pagnell – Olney road. The 14th century church of All Saints' is very fine and inside is a brass portrait of John Mordon who was rector here under Henry V.

On the outskirts of the village, partly a conservation area, there lies Emberton Country Park which has a mile of frontage along the banks of the Ouse and four lakes.

Fenny Stratford

➤ Browne Willis, LL D, missed knowing his grandfather, Thomas Willis, MD, by a mere seven years. His grandfather had died in 1675 and he himself had not been born until 1682. Yet his love and pride in his ancestor was a ruling factor in his life.

True, he had every right to be proud of him. Thomas had been a celebrated physician and surgeon to Charles II and had made important contributions to the knowledge of the structure and functions of the brain, and also delved into the mysteries of diabetes. He had purchased Whaddon Hall from the Duke of Buckingham, although he chose not to live there himself, and permanently resided in St Martin's Lane, London, where he died.

Chances are that he in turn would have been proud of his grandson, for Browne Willis became a famous antiquarian, turning out during his lifetime nearly 1,000 volumes of closely written manuscripts, though it was said his handwriting was so atrocious that even he could not read it. He was one of the founder members of the Society of Antiquarians and Member of Parliament for Buckingham. He married, had a family, and lived at Whaddon Hall, which he loved. Though eccentric, he was generous to a fault and to his own detriment.

He developed an absolute fascination for church buildings and rebuilt the church at Fenny Stratford in 1724–30, in which his simple tomb may be seen. As was his nature, he contributed most of the money towards the rebuilding himself and the remainder was raised by subscription. In 1866 a large nave was added, thereby making the church of Browne Willis into its north aisle, and a further south aisle was added in 1908.

Whilst all the excitement of the building of the church was going on, his grandfather was still uppermost in the mind of Browne Willis and when he laid the foundation stone and the church was consecrated, he chose St Martin of Tours as its Patron Saint, after St Martins Lane and the fact that both his grandfather and father died on St Martin's Day. He also placed a picture of his grandfather in the church with a suitable inscription.

He then did a most unusual thing. He required that a Divine Service should be held every St Martin's Day followed by a dinner. Even more unusual, he then gave to the church six small pieces of ordnance or cannon with instructions that they were to be fired also on every St Martin's Day. All this was to honour his grandfather and parents.

The six pieces of ordnance are known as the 'Fenny Poppers', stored on a shelf in the church, and fired annually in accordance with his wishes. They look for all the world like quart pots and are made of gunmetal. They stand roughly seven inches high and weigh every bit of twenty pounds each. They are three and a half inches in diameter at the muzzle and four inches in diameter at the breech. In the time of Browne Willis, they needed to be charged with 'four ounces of shilling gunpowder.'

Today they are still stuffed with gunpowder then, using wooden pegs, newspaper is rammed in, leaving a touch-paper. Meanwhile a heated rod (it must be stressed of great length) is prepared which, when ready, is applied to the touch paper and – bang! The noise of the firing of the 'Fenny Poppers' has been heard in Olney some twelve miles away!

Browne Willis would be pleased indeed to know that his last wishes were still being adhered to in this most unusual custom. He died in 1760, a poor man, having given away nearly all he had.

On Watling Street, about one mile north east of Fenny Stratford, stands the Denbigh Bridge bearing a plaque stating that, prior to September 1838, passengers on the railway for Birmingham were forced to alight here and proceed in a horsedrawn coach by road to Rugby, where they rejoined the railway for the remainder of the journey. As soon as the London to Birmingham railway was completed in 1838, this slight inconvenience ceased.

Fingest

Bishop Henry Burgwash was a nasty piece of work and it was unfortunate that Fingest was landed with him. He was described as 'neither good for church nor state, sovereign nor subjects' and furthermore was 'covetous, rebellious, ambitious and injurious'. Nevertheless, these personal attributes seem to have been just those qualities needed for promotion in the Church of the 14th century for he was twice Lord Treasurer, once Chancellor and once Ambassador to Bavaria.

At that time, the Bishop of Lincoln owned the manor of Fingest and the manor house, the remains of which are at the rear of the church, famous for its large Norman tower with twin saddle-back roof. The manor house was by all accounts small, unpretentious and homely compared to the Bishop's other capacious residences, which is perhaps why it proved so popular a home for prelates. In this lovely part of the Chilterns, it was also sheltered and out of the way, which is perhaps why our Henry preferred it to any other. Whereas some of his fellows came to meditate, he came to hunt in the woods, partake of the excellent food and wine, and generally have a good time, his every whim catered for by the locals.

It was in 1330 that he performed the most foul deed that brought poverty and want to the people of this quiet village. He enclosed some of the common lands into his new park, thus robbing the people of its use as somewhere for their cattle and sheep to graze, and leaving very little arable land to support them. It was galling for the villagers 'seeing their own bread, beef and mutton turned into the Bishop's venison and they durst not contest with him as he was Chancellor of England' and Henry did not care how much he rubbed it in. He indulged thoroughly in a life of idleness, luxury and greed.

He did not change even up to the time he died in 1340 and, although the villagers were still left minus their common land, they were pleased to see him go.

But this is not the end of the story. One night a resident from the manor house, who had known Henry Burgwash when he was alive, was walking up by the woods on part of that common land taken from the people when, to his utter astonishment and dismay, he encountered the ghost of the Bishop. As if this was not shock enough, Burgwash was clad as a Forester in a green tunic and, of all things, hose, and he was carrying bows, arrows and a bugle horn, which garb, of course, was not seemly to a man of such previous high standing in the Church.

When the poor fellow had calmed down somewhat, Burgwash poured out his troubles. It seemed that his rascally enclosure of the common land of Fingest had offended God to such a degree that he was condemned to act as keeper to that land. Every night he was required to trudge the bounds and would enjoy no peace of mind until the stolen property had been restored to its rightful owners, namely the people. He begged his friend on bended knee to do something about it and go as quickly as possible to the Canons at Lincoln and request them, in his name, to have the park reduced to its former extent and restore all the land he had taken.

The poor, frightened fellow went immediately to Lincoln and, surprisingly, the Canons for reasons best known to themselves, perhaps through guilt or from a natural wish not to encounter Henry Burgwash in any shape or form, arranged for the land to be properly restored.

The park was reduced to its proper size and the villagers received back their common, and it was alleged that the ghost of the Bishop was encountered no more. But perhaps there was something else Henry was paying for, as it is still said that sometimes on a dark night a figure in green has been seen riding 'wild-eyed' around the woods and lanes.

Fulmer

➤ Arthur Mee, writing in 1940, called it 'Arcadia', and one could not really dispute it, even today. It is amazing that, with such an extensive built-up area within so short a distance, Fulmer should remain an attractive village, retaining its setting of beautiful countryside, especially as it lies between two motorways, the M25 and the M40. It nestles snugly in a hollow beside the river Alderbourne on the road from Gerrards Cross to Wexham and, in its winding street, has all the necessary ingredients of a typical English village; Victorian and Georgian houses and cottages, the Black Horse Pub and a well-used Village Hall, not forgetting the Church of St James.

This pretty church was built by Sir Marmaduke Dayrell in 1610 and is thought to be only the second church to be built in the whole of England following the Reformation. Sir Marmaduke was Lord of the Manor, lived at Fulmer Place, and was a man of distinction. There is a splendid monument to him in a deep arched recess in the chancel where lies his recumbent figure clad in armour, with that of his wife just a little beyond and above, whilst their children kneel in profile in front. Inscribed thereon is the information that he was 'Servant to ye famous Queen Elizabeth in her warres both by sea and land and after in her Household.' He was also cofferer to James I and Charles I, and 'favoured by all these renowned princes and employed in matters of great trust for the space of fifty years.' Quite a testimonial!

St James was consecrated on 1st November 1610 by Doctor Barlow, then Bishop of Lincoln, in the presence of the founder, Sir Marmaduke, and a great congregation. All walked the churchyard with great ceremony prior to Sir Marmaduke entering the church between two Knights. The Bishop then asked him if he renounced all rights to the church, whereupon Sir Marmaduke replied that he did so both willingly and joyfully. It was a lengthy ceremony and may be found described in great detail in Volume II of the Records of Buckinghamshire.

The Black Horse Public House next door was at that time merely a hut or hostel used by the masons and other workmen during the building of the church.

The church was restored by Street in 1877–84, when the chancel was rebuilt and the south aisle added.

Richard Eskrigge, High Sheriff of the County, built another Fulmer Place on the site of the old one in the 18th century. His grandson, Richard Owen, was a rich merchant who transacted business with Napoleon, which included many fat contracts for the supply of the French troops at St Dominique. As with most ventures, events cannot be foreseen and, during the war with England, Napoleon was quick to repudiate all his English debts, which ruined poor Owen. He was forced to part with Fulmer Place and died a heartbroken man.

His son was Richard Owen (1804–92), the eminent Zoologist, who nursed a longing for the Fulmer Place of his childhood and hoped one day to regain it. Alas, it was not to be, but he does mention in his letters how, years later, he paid a nostalgic visit back to his ancestral home and whilst wandering in the grounds, amid his father's fishponds, he plucked a leaf from an apple tree for his sister and was suddenly confronted by the owner who, upon hearing who he was, welcomed him into his home.

Gawcott

➤ The church of Holy Trinity at Gawcott, a small hamlet some two miles south of Buckingham, is in the classical Georgian style and was designed by the incumbent, the Reverend Thomas Scott, in 1827. He was in turn the second son of that other Reverend Thomas Scott of Aston Sandford, and the father of the great Victorian architect, Sir Gilbert Scott, who was born here in 1811.

Thomas Scott, junior, had been curate at Emberton before becoming perpetual curate at Gawcott. In Bledlow church he married Euphemia Lynch of Antigua, who was related to Sir

Humphrey Gilbert, half brother to Sir Walter Raleigh, hence the reason they gave the name Gilbert to their son.

The young Gilbert Scott was a happy little boy and, left to his own devices, loved nothing better than sketching and art in general. He watched with interest as the foundations of his father's new church were laid and he developed a fascination for architecture, particularly Gothic. He became very attached to Mr Jones, his art master who, despite the fact that his work had been much admired in his youth by no less a personage than Sir Joshua Reynolds, was a humble and unambitious character. Mr Jones visited his pupil twice a week and in later life Gilbert was to recollect how he awaited to see 'with heart-felt joy, his art master's loose drab gaiters coming through the bushes' knowing that they would be going off together perhaps to sketch the church at Hillesden or the Early English architecture of Chetwode.

His book *Recollections of My Life* holds a delightful miscellany of some of the colourful, everyday characters of the Gawcott of his boyhood. He mentions that all the women made the Buckinghamshire lace and in the cottages was a vertical post revolving on an axis, with a wooden arm, to which toddlers were secured, so that they could run around the kitchen while the mother plodded on working unhindered at her lace pillow.

When Gilbert left Gawcott, it was to take up an apprenticeship in architecture and, as his term was drawing to an end, he sadly lost his father. Soon after he received a commission to build Union Workhouses at Amersham and Buckingham which were required under the Poor Law Act of 1834.

In 1844 he won an open competition for a great church at Hamburg in Germany and became a most prolific worker. His prodigious output during his lifetime included the building or restoration of 38 cathedrals, 474 churches and approximately 200 secular buildings, including St Pancras Station and the Albert Memorial, after which he was knighted by Queen Victoria and commissioned by her to do more work at Windsor. He became Professor of Architecture at the Royal Academy and lectured with brilliance.

He gave of his best in the restoration of many Buckinghamshire churches, but surely the commission that must have afforded him most pleasure was to restore the magnificent church at Hillesden that he had so dearly loved as a boy.

Not only did Sir Gilbert Scott have connections with the county through his father and grandfather, but he also had an uncle, Samuel King, who had the living at Latimer and Gilbert often went to stay with him. He largely rebuilt the church at that village and it is well worth a visit.

Towards the end of his life, his thoughts returned again and again to the little hamlet of his boyhood, and he remembered Mr Churchwarden Law, who dined every Sunday at the Vicarage, becoming so bewildered and confused by the number of cruets at table that he sprinkled his meat with sugar, giving much merriment to Gilbert and his brothers and sisters.

He died in 1888 and it seems a long way from Gawcott to the mighty Westminster Abbey where he now sleeps, yet he is forever remembered through his work in the many Buckinghamshire churches he so lovingly restored.

Gayhurst

It is a pity that young Everard Digby concerned himself with religious politics, for he had everything going for him. He was tall, handsome and accomplished, particularly in the fields of swordsmanship and music, and these personal assets led to him being dubbed 'the finest gentleman in England'.

Born in the late 16th century, he had married whilst in his 'teens', and his wife had inherited the manor of Gayhurst amid lovely countryside some two miles north-west of Newport Pagnell. His first son was born in 1603, the same year he was knighted by James I. Fortune certainly seemed to favour him, and yet he sat brooding in his splendid Gayhurst House.

He had received his education from Romish priests and

later had made a friend of Father Gerard, who would some-times visit Gayhurst. Times had been hard for Catholics, who were fined heavily and suffered persecution. Digby, and others, had hoped that, with the accession of King James, things would be easier for them. After all, had not King James' own mother, Mary, Queen of Scots, died a martyr to the cause. But the King had been brought up a Protestant, seeing very little of his mother, and what he had seen did not particularly impress him. Furthermore, he actively disliked the papacy. Suffice it to say, things did not improve and the Catholics were severely disappointed, especially when a law was passed requiring all Catholic priests to leave the country.

It was a day in October 1605 that Everard Digby met Robert Catesby, fervent in the Catholic cause, who had a definite charismatic charm about him. He gave Digby the outline of what was later to be known as the Gunpowder Plot, and went so far as to ask him to help defray the cost of the gunpowder etc. Digby agreed.

It must have been shortly after this that Guy Fawkes and others in the plot visited Gayhurst and they talked in a secret chamber especially constructed by a friend of Father Gerard for the purpose. In one of the apartments was a movable floor which, as described by Lipscomb, 'revolved on a pivot, which by a secret bolt, disclosed underneath it another room.' This room received light from a mullioned window which could only be seen from outside the house and then only from a great distance. Plotters going to and fro could not be observed even by those in the house, and there were many secret cupboards and drawers for papers.

In November, Digby set out for the Dun Cow Inn at Dunsmore Heath where he was to meet with others rallying under the disguise of a hunting party. On receiving news of the successful explosion in Westminster, this party were to capture Princess Elizabeth, the King's daughter. But early on the morning of 5th November, Catesby galloped up with the news that Guy Fawkes had been caught with the lighted taper in his hand and the plot foiled. However, he went on to completely mislead the party when he said that despite the setback, the country was in such a mood that if they carried on they would get massive support in Wales. Digby and about 40 others rode 80 miles in one night. Then he realised what a mistake it was. They would never receive support, and all the Gunpowder Plot had done was to make things worse for the Catholics in England. He decided to give himself up to the Sheriff of Warwickshire, a family friend, but whilst riding through a wood accompanied by his page and servant with this purpose in mind, he was surrounded by the Sheriff of Worcestershire's men who, shouting 'Here he is', leaped upon them. Digby replied with icy calm 'Here he is indeed. What then?'.

He was taken to the Tower where at first he maintained he had not been privy to the plot but had given £1,500 to finance it, and he steadfastly refused to give the names of any involved. However, at his trial he pleaded guilty and on 30th January 1606, he was dragged on a hurdle to St Paul's churchyard where he was hanged, drawn and quartered. This procedure called for the executioner of a traitor to remove the body from the gallows before life was extinct, then to pluck out the heart and hold it aloft crying 'Here is the heart of a traitor!' It is said that when the executioner held up the heart of Sir Everard making the same declaration, Sir Everard called out 'Thou liest!', which gave everyone something of a turn, not the least being the executioner.

His widow and children lived on at Gayhurst where his two sons grew to manhood and both were knighted. The eldest, Sir Kenelm, turned out to be one of the most remarkable men of his age and was endowed with his father's good looks, charm and talents. Through him and his brother John, who was killed in the service of the King at the Battle of Langport in 1645, the family overcame its misfortune and regained its former honours. Kenelm married Venetia Stanley whom he adored.

When visiting Gayhurst, you may happen to come across some particularly succulent snails, said to be still abundant in watery places, woods and mud walls. They are edible and were brought over from France by Sir Kenelm for use by his Lady Venetia as a restorative against consumption. This snail, known as the Pomatium, is identified by its flesh which is said to be particularly firm and is white tinged with red.

Gayhurst House later came into the hands of the Wright family and was remodelled by them in 1728. In the same year George Wright also rebuilt the church of St Peter which is an important example of the Classical style.

Gerrards Cross

In the beginning their name was Shobbington, this family that lived between Hedgerley and Gerrards Cross, and their chief seat was on land now known as Bulstrode Park. They had lived there for generations, long before the coming of the Normans, and they had something of a reputation for being fearless fighters. They had heard all about the mighty William the Conqueror and Harold's defeat at Hastings, but they had remained more or less untouched. That is until William decided to hand over their park and estate to one of his nobles. This aroused their fighting spirit and Old Shobbington, the head of the family, resolved that he would rather die on the spot than part with his family possessions, a resolution heartily endorsed by all his kin. They had a considerable number of tenants and servants and these they armed to the hilt. When the Norman who had been granted their estate became aware of this, he immediately prepared to take the estate by force.

The crisis escalated when in turn this news reached the ears of Old Shobbington, who applied to his friends and relations living nearby. The Penns and Hampdens took arms and came to his aid.

This local army threw up entrenchments and dug themselves in, whilst the Normans encamped in the valley below. The Shobbingtons decided that the best form of defence was attack and sallying forth at night, mounted on bulls, they charged the enemy camp. Needless to say, the Normans were surprised and terror-stricken. Many of them were killed and the rest fled as if the hounds of hell were after them. When William received news of this, he was uncertain as to what course should be taken. This heroic stand by one family had caused quite a stir and he sent for Shobbington, promising him safe conduct if he would come to London and discuss the matter. The invitation was accepted and Shobbington rode to the King on a bull followed by his seven sons, also on bulls. The sight must have caused quite a stir in London.

The family from Buckinghamshire were not in the least awed in the presence of the King and when he asked Old Shobbington how he dared to resist him when the rest of the country had not, Shobbington told him of the length of time the estate in question had been owned by his people and suggested that if William would permit them to keep it, he would become his subject and be ever faithful to him. The bargain was struck and the victorious Shobbingtons returned to their lands – but from thenceforth many called them Shobbington Bulstrode and gradually the first name disappeared, leaving just the name Bulstrode.

The medieval history of Bulstrode is somewhat hazy and in the 13th and 14th centuries it was in turn owned by the Abbey of Burnham and then the Abbey of Bisham, but after the Reformation, the gallant little Bulstrode family were once more in possession.

Sir Richard Bulstrode, who was a good man, and brilliant lawyer and author, remained loyal to the Stuarts no matter what and even at 80 years old accompanied James II to France. He died at the Court of St Germains at the ripe old age of 101.

The infamous Judge Jeffreys bought the manor and built a mansion there in 1686. He was a most unpopular man and, as his mansion was built of reddish brick, it was said by the people to be 'bloodstained'. It appears there was a fire which caused Jeffreys to remove to Chalfont St Peter and the manor was then sold to the Portland family.

The third Duke of Portland was a well-known minister in the reign of George III and his Duchess created a famous museum at Bulstrode and was the owner of the celebrated Portland Vase, which has recently been repaired and placed on show.

The atmosphere became perhaps more political when the fourth Duke was Prime Minister and the road to Bulstrode was a busy one with dispatches and famous people. The road is still busy as it skirts the estate but that wonderful victory against the mighty Conqueror by local people will never be forgotten.

Gibraltar

➤ It was in 1970 that Gibraltar was handed over without a shot being fired.

This kind of headline startled even the calmest of newspaper readers until they read on that the Gibraltar referred to was the tiniest of Buckinghamshire hamlets and that it was handed over from the parish of Cuddington to the parish of Dinton. And, it may well be asked, where is it?

Let the 'Bottle and Glass' be your marker on the Aylesbury – Thame road, an attractive 15th century inn with dormer windows peeping from deep thatch, like eyes from under beetle brows. Down the side runs a little lane where cluster some 16 cottages, mostly of thatch, amid a sea of blossom in spring. This is Gibraltar, a small community, so named because it stands on a slab of rock as solid as that famous rock at the gateway to the Mediterranean. Attempts to dig down to any great depth have proved fruitless due to this impenetrable stone. For years Gibraltar was unmarked and unsignposted. Now there is just a finger pointing in its direction.

John Milton was not the only one to leave London to come to Buckinghamshire during the horrors of the Great Plague of 1665. It is said that 80 refugees walked from London to Gibraltar where a relative of one of the group lived and here they settled. But unfortunately they had unwittingly carried the Plague with them, for only a day after their arrival, a child sickened with it and 40 deaths among them ensued. The contagion took quite a time to clear and one can imagine that this small hamlet must have been 'out of bounds' to the surrounding countryside.

Nearly 200 years later, misfortune struck again, when there was an epidemic of cholera in various parts of the county. It was reported in August 1849 that the cholera had appeared at Gibraltar and Dinton and that several cases had proved fatal. Two days later the people of Gibraltar had left their cottages and were living in tents some distance off to avoid the contagion. Despite this, there is a tablet in Cuddington churchyard wall which was erected by the Medical Officer of the parish 'to the memory of 48 persons, residents of Gibraltar, who were cut off in August 1849 after a few hours illness by Asiatic Cholera.'

One family escaped the scourge and put it firmly down to the fact that they had hung up in their cottage a string of onions. When they went to use them, they were found to be in a rotting condition, due to the fact, they averred, that the disease had attacked the onions instead of the household.

After that, happily, there was no trouble until 1970 when the people of Gibraltar, population 40, drew up and presented a petition to the County Council stating that, as most of their interests were in the village of Dinton (particularly the Women's Institute), they wished to be transferred from the parish of Cuddington to the parish of Dinton. The County Council must have gasped. As is well known, it is usually a tedious, lengthy process to even begin to effect this important kind of territorial transfer, with a local inquiry, the Minister himself being called upon to make a decision, and an Order having to be made. What is more, parish boundary maps have to be altered. In any event, would Cuddington want to relinquish Gibraltar peaceably and, even more to the point, would Dinton want to accept it?

Relations between the two villages remained calm and, suffice it to say, gallant little Gibraltar won the day and is now included in the parish of Dinton, to the satisfaction of all parties.

Granborough Village Hall

Granborough

➤ Or Grandborough, that is the question. Some of the guide books insert the 'd' but the majority, including the County Guide, does not. Eland says that the original place name was Green Burgh, or hill, which speaks for itself.

It is a small village that stands in extensive pastures between North Marston and Winslow, with a most unusual village hall built in 1910 that has the attractive feature of an upper floor verandah.

The 14th century church of St John the Baptist houses a 15th century alabaster panel some 15 inches high carved with the Crucifixion and now under glass. It was found built into a gable of a farm in the village.

The people of Granborough seem to have been very adept at hiding things away for in the last century a pewter chrismatory was found, this time built into a niche of a wall of the church. A chrismatory was a vessel which held the holy oils and was used prior to the Reformation in the ceremonies of Baptism, Confirmation and Extreme Unction and, therefore, played a vital part in Church ritual. Came the Reformation and articles such as this were sought and destroyed. It is quite pleasing to think that whilst clerks were going around making inventories and collecting valuable church items, under their very noses, some hand was secreting this treasure away.

The original has been removed to the Museum of Christchurch Cathedral at Oxford for safe keeping, but in the church today can be seen a faithful copy. It is roughly six inches long, made of pewter with lion's feet, and it has three receptacles for the sacramental oils.

Although the month of May, the writer felt a considerable wave of warmth whilst standing in the aisle and turned to find an old fashioned iron stove glowing away, and another one near the chancel, their narrow pipe chimneys travelling far up into the timbered roof.

Great Hampden

There was tremendous excitement in the locality when the news came through that Queen Elizabeth I was to visit old Griffith Hampden, grandfather to John, at Hampden House. Preparations were started days, even weeks, before to ensure that the Queen received every comfort. Griffith considered this visit a great honour to his family. They had held estates here since the Conquest, maybe even before that, and as she stepped from her carriage, he welcomed her with great gallantry. He was proud to show her over his house, which had been built in the 14th century and stood just the other side of a carriage way to the church.

Eventually, he conducted her to her chamber, whereupon the great Queen looked from the window and declared what a pity it was that any kind of a view was hindered by so many trees. Griffith bowed her Goodnight and withdrew. Immediately the door closed, he rounded up all his estate workers, plus anyone else he could lay his hands on, and, whilst the Queen slept, this workforce hewed down a tremendous number of trees.

Came the dawn, when the Queen's curtains were drawn, she beheld the most magnificent vista, a wide avenue between elms, sweet chestnuts, and beech right down to Hampden Bottom. Was it really a surprise to her, or had she lain awake all night listening to the noise of the axes and the crashing to earth of the giant trees?

Later, at the bottom of this splendid avenue, which became known as the Queen's Gap, two lodges were built, one each side of the drive. The best view of them is obtained from the Missenden-Risborough road along Hampden Bottom. They are named 'the pepperpots' or 'boxes' for that is just what they look like. Perhaps with a stretch of the imagination, they could have been called 'the condiments'. Be that as it may, up until a few years ago, each of these pepperpots consisted of one room only, one being the kitchen-cum-sitting room and over the other side of the drive, the bedroom. It was a sight to behold at a certain time in the evening when the tenants, a little old lady and gentleman, bearing a candle and wearing nightgowns and caps, crossed the drive to the other pepperpot to bed.

Now these lodges have been extended, but despite this, they will be forever known to the local people as 'the pepperpots'.

Great Kingshill

Both Great Kingshill and the Royal Oak stand on the A4128 leading from Prestwood to the top of Cryers Hill, that runs down to the lovely Hughenden Valley. The pub backs on to a village green and/or common, where cricket is played in summer and not so old men sit and watch in complete relaxation.

There was a time, not so long ago, when this part of the country, with Prestwood and Holmer Green, became a vision in spring with line upon line of cherry blossom showing up against the blue sky. But progress came in the shape of development and with it went the cherry orchards and the customs that belonged to them; the delectable Cherry Pie Feasts, for instance.

Although the village now consists mostly of modern dwellings, they blend in pleasantly with the older brick and flint cottages left over from the last century and today beautifully maintained. Opposite the village hall, the Royal Oak is also of brick and flint with a modern extension at the rear. There are two bay windows at the front and a shallow canopy supported by eight stout posts. On the outside wall on the northern side of the building, at the level of the upper floor, there is the outline of two figures created out of beer bottle bottoms set into the split flints. Some four to five feet in height, they have something of a 'Lowry' look about them. Anyone passing along the road, walking or driving, must surely notice this most unusual feature. The head of one figure is filled in and the other open. Whether this is intended to denote a variation in sex is not known.

Parts of the Royal Oak go back some 300 years and the name has changed several times. Once it was known as 'The Adam and Eve' and then again as 'The Two Junipers', so who the bottle people are meant to represent is anyone's guess. But there is something so jaunty and jolly about them and, although their outline is of the briefest, they seem alive and welcoming. Certainly the best of advertisements for a pub and something singular in the county of Buckingham.

It is difficult to find a guide book that mentions the Kingshills (Great and Little), which is sad, for make no mistake they are both very desirable places in which to live.

Great Missenden

It is surprising how few of the many books written on the Chilterns and the county make mention of the 16th century manorial courthouse which lies in a courtyard through the coach arch of the George Inn in the High Street, opposite Church Street. The inn was built in 1480 and the courthouse was in use right up to the beginning of this century.

It is a long black and white half-timbered building with an overhanging upper storey and, in times past, had an exterior staircase to an upper room. There is an original mullioned window (now blocked) at the north-east end and there are heavy ceilinged beams on the ground floor with curved struts and the upper roof has queen-post trusses with braced tie beams.

The manorial court, or Court Leet, sat mostly under the lord himself or, if he was indisposed, his steward. Here petty justice was done and all the affairs of the manor and copyhold tenants were attended to. Disputes were settled, rents paid, and open fields and common pastures policy was discussed and protected together with the farming community as a whole. The Court was open – all might attend – and this provided something of a safeguard against the lord becoming too oppressive or tyrannical, if the mood ever took him.

It is always rewarding to take a stroll down Great Missenden High Street with its 17th and 18th century buildings and pleasant shops, and even more so to take in this old courthouse, a reminder of the manorial justice of long ago.

Grendon Underwood

The two constables in the 16th century, whilst performing their duties in keeping law, order and the peace, could not have been exactly overworked in a village the size of Grendon Underwood. Yet the village was a thoroughfare from the northern parts of Oxfordshire, which was why the roads were in such an appalling condition during the winter months. And then, of course, there was the grassy track that ran via Bernwode Forest and was frequented by gipsies, strolling players and the like on their way to and from London.

Whether their working lives were to any degree exciting or not, both officers were filled with righteous indignation one summer night when they came across a drunken lout asleep in the church porch. He was obviously one of those strolling players and, with much show of importance, they arrested him. Although they handled him roughly, he offered no physical resistance, but he certainly had a way with words.

They charged him with stealing from the church poor box, which he denied emphatically and, after much skilful argument, he insisted that they open the box, which certainly had not occurred to them. After seemingly an age of pomposity from them and a further deluge of words from him, they did so, and were forced to admit there was nothing missing. The lout then had the cool, calm nerve to turn around and tell them that they had made much ado about nothing.

They were only too thankful to release him and 'thanked God they were rid of a knave.' How could they have known, as they watched him go, that they would be immortalised as Dogberry and Verges, the two constables in *Much Ado About Nothing*.

Yes, you've guessed it – the drunken lout was none other than William Shakespeare who frequently drew on real life for character and dialogue in his plays.

The immortal Bard often travelled back and forth between London and his home at Stratford-upon-Avon, and it is said that, as he passed through Grendon Underwood, he always reckoned to stay at The Ship Inn. The inn is now a house, oak-framed with brick infilling, and has an oval window in a gable. This is said to be the attic room where the poet, looking out over forest land perhaps to 'a bank whereon the wild thyme grows', wrote *A Midsummer Night's Dream* and perhaps he imagined those fairy characters, Oberon, Puck and Bottom, flitting between the moonlit trees.

In its heyday, The Ship Inn could accommodate 40 people and the inn sign is now a prominent piece among the collection of the Bucks Archaeological Society at Aylesbury. On one side is depicted a Tudor ship in full sail, and on the other a view of the same ship from a different angle. Considering that this sign stood up to all kinds of weather for centuries, the colours are said to be quite beautiful.

These stories of Shakespeare at Grendon Underwood were part of a collection by John Aubrey, the antiquarian, who lived within 26 years of the death of Shakespeare and in fact claimed that he had met one of those very same constables, still alive though aged, when he visited the village in 1642 and that his name was Joseph Howe. It is true that the name Howe was prominent in Grendon Underwood at that time for the rector was Thomas Howe, and Aubrey also mentions a Mrs Howe of that village who sent food to the President of Trinity College, Oxford. It is quite likely that the constable was a member of this family.

The church porch in which Shakespeare is reputed to have slept is no more, but the mid 13th century doorway is remarkably fine and inside there is a touching monument in white marble by the Dutch artist, Scheemakers, to John Pigott 1751. The late Mr Pigott is seated wearing a Roman toga, and his son, who died at the tender age of 13 whilst at school, is depicted in profile on a medallion borne by a cherub. This memorial was erected by the sad wife and mother of both.

Halton

When the Rothschild family settled in Buckinghamshire in the 19th century, they built seven quite splendid mansions in the French and English traditions within an eight mile radius of Aylesbury – at Tring, Mentmore, Wing, Aston Clinton, Eythorpe, Waddesdon and Halton. They also vastly improved, expanded or rebuilt the villages around their gates, adding schools, libraries and generously supporting local charities. Halton, near Wendover, where the Chiltern escarpment rises sharply above the Aylesbury Plain and the hills reach their highest point, is a classic example.

Baron Lionel de Rothschild purchased the estate from Sir George Dashwood in 1853 and when he died in 1874, it passed to his son, Alfred, who built Halton mansion in 1884. It turned out to be a magnificent chateau with velvet lawns and sweeping drives, not to mention breathtaking views, where Alfred entertained the important personages of his day on the most lavish scale. Guests included such people as the Prince of Wales and Lily Langtry, and the Shah of Persia among many others. Alfred liked nothing better than to astonish his guests by tearing around the park in his small carriage which was pulled by a pair of zebra.

During the First World War, the park was used by the Army and the Royal Flying Corps and, on the death of Alfred in 1918, the whole of the estate was completely taken over by the Royal Air Force. The mansion itself is now the Officers' Mess, which must provide excellent incentive for promotion from the ranks.

The village is down a turning off the A4011 and is both quaint and pretty. It still retains a Victorian picture postcard look with its half-timbered cottages and houses, some with tall twisted 'barley sugar' chimneys rising amid tall trees. On some may be seen the five arrows of the Rothschild family crest and their motto – 'Concord Industry and Integrity'. But the most interesting and intriguing are the decorative plaster plaques that appear on some of the buildings. For instance, four of these are to be seen on the old post office – one depicts a girl carrying fruit, another throwing corn to chickens, and there is a harvester and a skater. Apparently, Alfred de Rothschild was very fond of skating.

On other cottages are to be found plaques with woodcutting and harvesting scenes. Yet more plaques showing owls, a cock and a reaper can be seen on a lodge along the road to Weston Turville.

Many workmen were brought over from the Continent by the Rothschilds for the building of their houses, and it is thought that these delightful, unusual plaques were made by foreign craftsmen.

Hambleden

The picture conjured up of the famous Cardinal Wolsey getting into his bed, is perhaps not a pretty one, but his carved oak bedhead was incredibly beautiful. Part of it stands in the church of St Mary the Virgin at Hambleden and now forms an altar in the south transept. It is a splendid piece of early 16th century Renaissance panelling and its eight panels are richly carved with men, angels, monsters, foliage and the arms of Cardinal Wolsey surmounted by a Cardinal's hat, and also those of Richard Fox, Bishop of Winchester (1501–1528). Wolsey succeeded Fox in this post.

Just how it came to Hambleden is something of an enigma. One school of thought is that it may have come from The Vyne, near Basingstoke, the home of the Sandys family, who often entertained Cardinal Wolsey and Bishop Fox. Elizabeth Sandys married Ralph Scrope of Hambleden and came to live at the manor house, and it is suggested that she may have brought her bed with her.

On the other hand, it may have been purchased at the sale of the Bishop of Lincoln's manor house at Fingest some 100 years ago by a very popular rector of Hambleden (Canon W. H. Ridley), who brought it back and fixed it to the back of the vestry cupboard in the church. Whatever and wherever, it is truly magnificent to behold.

The church has undergone much restoration over the centuries, but nevertheless the end result is particularly beautiful. It is a large, airy building with an ancient 12th century font at which Thomas Cantelupe (1218–1282), Bishop of Hereford and native of Hambleden, was baptised. This font has the remains of clamps that once secured the lid in order to prevent theft of the consecrated water, which was often used as a 'livener' in the brew of witches!

In the north transept, in alabaster, and to which some of the original colours still cling, kneel Sir Cope D'Oyley and his wife, Martha, gazing into each other's eyes for all eternity. They died in the early 18th century and beneath them kneel all ten of their offspring. Those who carry skulls predeceased their parents.

In front of this remarkable memorial stands the great oak muniment chest that once was the property of James Brudenell, seventh Earl of Cardigan, who was born and baptised in Hambleden, and who led the heroic Charge of the Light Brigade into 'the valley of death' at the Battle of Balaclava

(1854) during the Crimean War. It is said the chest accompanied him at this time. It is large and weighty and must have brought forth expletives from whoever had the job of carrying it around!

The name of Hambleden means 'village in a valley' and this most attractive of villages certainly lives up to its name. The surrounding hills provide a backcloth of rising, thick woods of varying shades of green. The parish is bounded on the north by the river Thames and along its banks can be seen 'Greenlands', once the house of the first Viscount Hambleden, better known as W. H. Smith, bookseller and stationer.

The village green is encircled by the church and quaint cottages, some of brick and flint. The manor house is early 17th century whilst the rectory is of the 18th century.

A leisurely stroll through the village brings you to the Stag and Hounds and a solitary old-fashioned butcher's shop with a Victorian knife-grinder and sausage or mince machine in the window.

Hanslope

'If Hanslope spire were ten times higher
I'd take off my shoe and jump over it.'

➤ This is one of those rhymes with a catch in it that has been repeated to Buckinghamshire children for generations and quite often has them transfixed with boredom. It refers to the spire of Hanslope church, which is not only the highest in the county (186 ft) but also the most graceful and is conspicuous for many miles around. It is said that seven counties may be seen from its apex on which stands a model of a whippet dog as a weathervane. There was a time when the spire was even higher, 200 ft, but it was struck by lightning in 1804, and after repairs, it lost a few feet.

Around 200 years ago there lived a man called Robert Cadman, a famous steeplejack, who repaired many of the high steeples in England. He was called in to repair the steeple of Hanslope church. He refused a ladder, as was his wont, and climbed to the top, where he played a triumphant tattoo on the little drum he always carried on his back for that purpose. He then hung the drum around the weathervane, executed the necessary repairs, climbed down and spent the evening at a certain hostelry in the village where he became more than a little happy and appreciative of the local ale. In the middle of his umpteenth pint, he suddenly remembered he had left his drum at the very top of the church spire and to the consternation of his new found friends at the inn, he insisted that he must climb up to rescue his beloved little instrument. Happily the villagers managed to persuade him against this course and it was not until the next morning that he climbed the tower once again and recovered his drum. Several years later he fell from a church tower and was killed.

The village of Hanslope with its wide streets and stone cottages has something of a Midlands look and sometimes the close proximity of the Northamptonshire border has proved very convenient.

In the early part of the 19th century, prizefighting was a most popular sport with all levels of society, who mingled together for the excitement of seeing two men fight barefisted and to wager money on the outcome. It was also illegal, and when in June 1830 a match was arranged by men of honour at a dinner at the Castle Tavern, Holborn between Alexander McKay, the champion of all Scotland, and the notorious Irishman, Simon Byrne, for the enormous sum of £100 a side, to take place at Hanslope, the efforts and activities of the Buckinghamshire Law Officers together with local Constable Evans, knew no bounds. They kept such a close watch on McKay, who was staying at the Watts Arms in the village, and also anyone they suspected of being connected with the proposed fight, that the situation was impossible.

It was decided, therefore, to change the venue of the match to Salcey Green just over the Northamptonshire border. All was set for the 2nd June and, on that morning the difficulty was how to get the Scottish champion out of the Watts Arms unseen. The landlord's niece saved the day by creating a diversion by dancing out of the front door in a kilt. Today this event would not cause even the batting of an eye, but in those days it was a singular occurrence, and took everyone's mind off any thought of prize fights. Whilst this was going on, McKay was smuggled out of the bar window into Long Street, and taken just over the border to Salcey Green.

The bareknuckled fight lasted a tortuous 47 rounds and a round was not a set time as it is today. It was just a fresh start after a fall when a man was given just 30 seconds to recover, and if his seconds did not bring him to the scratch point in the middle of the ring by that time, he was considered defeated. This must be where the expression 'come up to scratch' came from.

Poor McKay lost and was carried unconscious back to his bedroom at the Watts Arms. He died the next day at the tender age of 26 years.

The result of the fight became known to the Law and Simon Byrne was arrested on board the Dublin packet at Liverpool and a Bill of Indictment made out against him and Tom Cribb, one of McKay's seconds. As may be imagined, at the trial there was a tremendous amount of money and influence behind Byrne and he was ably represented by three distinguished lawyers of the day. The jury took only ten minutes to reach a verdict of 'Not Guilty' and the courtroom rang with cheers.

Despite objections from the vicar, McKay was buried in the churchyard at Hanslope and over his grave was added a sad little epitaph which ended:

> 'If you have ever fought before
> Determine now to fight no more.'

Hardwick

The first village outside Aylesbury on the way to Winslow, it stands on a rise just off the main road. It is well-grouped with cottages and houses clustered around the interesting Church of St Mary, which has some delightful windows. Parts of the nave are Anglo-Saxon. In the chancel is a memorial to Sir Robert Lee, who died in 1616, and was an ancestor of the famous Confederate Leader of the American Civil War, General Robert E. Lee. The family once held considerable estates in Hardwick and nearby Weedon.

From outside in the churchyard there are splendid views of the surrounding countryside that absolutely beg the visitor to sit on the seat provided and peacefully contemplate the prospect. Close to the south side of the tower may be found a rather surprising monument of stone placed there by Lord Nugent in 1818 to mark the spot where the bones of 247 persons were buried. These were discovered in that year in pits four to five feet deep at a place called Holman's Bridge just outside Aylesbury. From scrupulous examination and deliberation at the time it was concluded that these were the remains of both Royalist and Parliamentary troops who fell at the Battle of Aylesbury in November 1642. Lord Nugent, a distinguished historian and Member of Parliament, arranged for them to be carefully removed and interred in the churchyard at Hardwick.

Immediately after the Battle of Aylesbury, it was given out that casualties numbered 290. The drop to 247 could take into account those bodies taken away at the time by relatives for private burial, especially as some of the townspeople themselves played no small part in the battle.

It was on 1st November 1642 that Prince Rupert, the King's nephew, entered the town of Aylesbury at approximately 6 am with some 10,000 Royalist troops. He and his men had been having a high old time at the expense of the people of the Vale of Aylesbury, pillaging, despoiling and laying waste to the land. The conduct of Prince Rupert and his troops did not improve in the town itself and the inhabitants were made to suffer all kinds of outrage and indignity.

Mercifully, it was not long before he received news that Sir William Balfour was approaching from Stony Stratford at the head of some 6,000 Parliamentary foot and horse troops, and it was said the foot troops were under the command of Colonel Hampden. Rupert did not relish fighting within the town as he did not trust the townspeople, and also because his cavalry would be at a greater advantage in the open countryside. He moved out to meet them, leaving just a small force behind in town. He must have been somewhat cheered to find that the reported 6,000 Parliamentary troops turned out to be a mere 1,500 men.

He had proceeded no further than the brook about half a mile outside of town, where the ford had been swollen by heavy rains, when Balfour's horse and foot checked him. Impetuous Rupert charged across the ford, ploughed through the first two lines of enemy infantry, and plunged into the centre of the horse troops. There was a sharp conflict of hand to hand fighting – one furious throng of clashing swords and poleaxes. In but a few minutes, the Royalists were driven back across the stream where Rupert rallied. But then he received the full force of pistol fire from the other side. He and his forces fell back on the town, where the most amazing factor of this battle occurred. The townspeople, having gathered together whatever arms they could, rushed upon his rear guard. The Royalists were forced to retreat towards Thame with both Roundheads and townspeople slaughtering the hindmost.

The dead were buried at Holman's Brook where they fell – Royalist and Roundhead alike in one common grave – all Englishmen caught up in conflict. Lord Nugent ends his inscription on the monument at Hardwick:

'May the memory of the brave be respected and may our country never again be called to take part in contests such as these which this tablet records.'

High Wycombe

➤ It has often been said that a gentleman by the name of Robert Raikes began the Sunday school movement, but Hannah Ball had started her Sunday school in High Wycombe some eleven years before he founded his at Gloucester.

Hannah was born in the village of Naphill in 1733, one of a family of twelve. From the first she was drawn to children and looked after others as well as her own brothers and sisters. She enjoyed amusing and training them. When her sister in law died, she went to live with her brother in High Wycombe in order to care for his family.

It was in the year 1762 that something quite frightening happened to Hannah. During a ferocious storm, she became so terrified that literally 'the fear of God' was put into her and she thought she could hear 'the last trumpet'. She later described how she felt as if she were being 'crushed beneath the weight of her sins' and, from then on, she resolved to direct her life in a spiritual path and to serve the Church.

Which one, that was the question? She searched, listening to notable and dedicated preachers, but none seemed to satisfy her. Then it was announced that John Wesley was coming to preach at High Wycombe and, although he was scheduled to speak as early as 5 o'clock in the morning, Hannah determined to go. The moment she heard him she knew that this was it – this was what she had been waiting to hear. It was not long before she and Wesley were friends and correspondents, and letters from him to her, together with her journal are preserved.

Around this time an eligible, upright young man sought Hannah's hand in marriage, and she gave the proposal serious thought, but was dissuaded from accepting by her spiritual adviser as it was said the young man was a 'stranger to the true religion.' A hard decision for someone like Hannah to make with her love of children.

Those early Methodists did not have an easy life anywhere and High Wycombe was no exception. They were often persecuted and one gentleman went so far as to arrange for drums to be beaten outside their chapel during the entire length of the service, making it impossible for the congregation to hear, let alone follow.

Nothing daunted, the indomitable Hannah started her Sunday school in 1769 and so became the pioneer of a great movement. Though she taught the children in her own house on a Sunday afternoon, ably assisted by her sister,

Anne, the Sunday school was affiliated to the parish church, and Hannah made sure that after each session, the children were taken to the church. At one service, when the Reverend Williams made the remark that 'if any Arminian entered heaven, the angels would cease to sing', Hannah gathered her children and walked out, for this was not the sort of thing that she had taught them. She never returned but continued with her Sunday school.

The education received at those early Sunday schools was all that was available for some children. Hannah taught them to read and write and by so doing she laid the foundation for the primary education of the future.

Her health began to fade in 1788 and she found it difficult to get about. In his last letter to her John Wesley said 'Look up, my dear friend, the prize is before us, we are on the point of parting no more. In time and eternity you will be united with your ever affectionate brother, John Wesley.'

She died in 1792 and was buried at Stokenchurch. The building that was her little Sunday school is no more, but in the opulent Oak Room of the Town Hall, amid the greats of the county, there is a window dedicated to her memory.

Hillesden

One of the most out of the way places, it is only reached via the narrow, lengthy lane that passes through lush fields filled with sheep and lambs in early spring. Eventually a handful of cottages appear and around a bend looms the outstanding church of All Saints.

In the 15th century, this church had been allowed to fall into a sorry state of disrepair and in 1493 the monks of Notley Abbey rebuilt it, save for the tower. Today it is generally considered to be one of the finest examples of Perpendicular architecture in Buckinghamshire and certainly served as the main source of inspiration to the Victorian architect, Sir Gilbert Scott, who lived as a boy in the nearby village of Gawcott. He felt drawn to this building and often walked over to sketch its beautiful contours. A drawing of

The Tower of All Saints Church, Hillesden

his hangs in the vestry. Later on in his life, he was asked to undertake the restoration of the church and, knowing it so well, he did so with much pleasure and sensitivity.

But what a story this church, standing in this small, remote hamlet, could tell of a day in the early spring of 1644 when, together with Hillesden House almost adjoining, it came under siege from Oliver Cromwell himself and 2,000 of his men! And, if memory tends to fade, as the house is today no more than a faint trace in the nearby meadow, there are those holes in the thick, oak door made by Roundhead bullets to act as reminders.

At that time, Hillesden House was the home of Sir Alexander Denton and family. He and Sir Edmund Verney, the Standard Bearer, living at nearby Claydon House, were the only two important Buckinghamshire landowners to stand for the King. They were related in that Sir Edmund had married Margaret, the sister of Sir Alexander, a choice he never once regretted. Sir Alexander himself had married Mary Hampden, a cousin of John Hampden, 'the Patriot' and champion of the Parliamentary cause, who had died the preceding year from wounds received at the Battle of Chalgrove.

The military situation was that Parliamentary forces were at Aylesbury and Newport Pagnell where Sir Samuel Luke was Governor, and the Royalists stood possessed of the country from Oxford to Banbury. Standing as it did halfway between the two, Hillesden was in a prime position in the strategy of either side and Sir Alexander decided that it would be both prudent and practicable to fortify his house and the church against attack. Colonel Smith with some 200 men and five small cannons was sent to his aid from Headquarters at Oxford. It is said that 1,000 local men were hired to dig a defensive ditch half a mile in circumference around the house and church, and a large cannon was improvised from a hollow elm tree.

A small force of 300 horse and foot from Aylesbury attacked. They were easily repelled, but took back word of all the works that were underway at Hillesden, which reached the ears of no less a personage than Oliver Cromwell. Anxious that the defensive works should not be given time for completion, he set out with 2,000 men – Sir Samuel Luke approaching from the Gawcott direction. Cromwell and his men reached Steeple Claydon and stayed the night there, resting in readiness for the attack the next morning.

Meanwhile, back at Hillesden, much scrambling was going on to finish the work on the fortifications as, despite those 1,000 local men, the ditch was still rather shallow and could easily be crossed. Desperate attempts were made to fix the five cannons to the church and to bind the elm cannon with iron. The Royalists would have stood a good chance had they been given another week, but on the morning of 4th March, Colonel Smith awoke to find the house and church completely surrounded with no avenue of escape. Cromwell called for immediate unconditional surrender. This was unacceptable to Smith and Sir Alexander, and they and their men put up a fight resulting in several being killed on both sides. Some Royalists barricaded themselves in the church, hence the bullet holes in the door. After the second assault, the defenders offered to surrender upon promise of quarter.

The next few minutes were to show an interesting side to Oliver Cromwell. As Smith walked out, a Roundhead whisked away his hat. Oliver was all sympathy and embarrassment, assuring him that 'If I can discover the man who took your hat, he shall be punished', and courteously asked Smith in the meantime to accept his own. It is to be hoped it was the right size!

Sadly, the promise of quarter was not kept and some of the Royalists were put to death after surrender, and later buried in the churchyard. The house was ransacked and money and valuables found hidden in the wainscoting. It was then fired, the flames visible for miles around, and by the evening it was a smouldering ruin. Sir Alexander was arrested and later died in captivity. Strangely, his sister, Susan, married an officer of the besieging force by the name of Captain Jaconiah Abercrombie. Unfortunately, the marriage was shortlived. The Captain was killed at Boarstall the following year.

Now, all that remains is this remarkable church standing in splendid isolation in the tiny hamlet.

Hulcott

➤ The Reverend William Morgan was very fond of boasting that were it not for him the literary world of the 19th century would not have enjoyed the brilliant novels of the talented Bronte sisters and, when you come to think about it, he was right!

For he and Patrick Bronte, the father of the girls, had been young curates together, during which time they became close friends. Furthermore, it was due to William that Patrick first went to Yorkshire, where he was appointed curate in charge of St Peter's, Hartshead. Close by was Woodhead Grove school where William had already met and intended to marry the headmaster's daughter, Jane Fennell. One weekend, purely by chance, William persuaded Patrick to come with him to Jane's home and again, purely by chance, Jane's cousin, Maria Branwell, was staying there. She and Patrick were immediately attracted to one another and the upshot of it was – a double wedding. The two curates hit on the idea of conducting the marriage of one another. On 29th December, 1812, Patrick peformed the marriage of William and Jane with Maria acting as bridesmaid, after which William stepped forward and married Patrick to Maria with Jane acting as bridesmaid. But for the introduction and the wedding performed by William, who knows? Certainly William was very proud of being the uncle of the Bronte sisters.

It was many years later in 1851, in the company of his second wife, that he came to take up the living of the 14th century All Saints church at Hulcott, Jane having died some years before.

Lying as it does some three quarters of a mile off the Aylesbury-Leighton Buzzard road, the village can so easily be missed in this fascinating countryside of deep hollows and long views. Reached by a lane of trimmed hedges with wide fields on either side, it is a sequestered spot with tall trees shading and encircling a wide oval green surrounded by pretty cottages, a manor house, an old school and a rectory. It cannot have looked very different to the new parson.

Behind the small lychgate on the south side of the green is one of the quaintest churches in the county with weatherboarded turret, a weathercock on top and a porch that seems to snuggle down with determination into a most pleasant churchyard. On a day of sunshine in February when we visited, the churchyard was strewn with primroses in bloom and lambs gambolled in the meadows. At the rear of the church, under more tall trees, an ancient moat glistened still with water, and a stream called Thistlebrook borders the parish.

The lady at the bungalow down the lane was hanging out washing that flapped and billowed on the line as we asked for the key of the church. She handed over the most intriguing, lengthy key of ornate proportions that must have been used on the little door inside the church years before William Morgan came to Hulcott. She recalled the day when someone else had borrowed the key and forgotten to return it, which led to one of the most nerve-racking nights she had ever endured until she found it on the doorstep the next morning.

The key slipped into the lock with the habit of centuries and inside the small building the weatherboarded bell turret is clearly seen to be supported by visible strong uprights and timbers.

Benedict Lee, a member of the famous Buckinghamshire family, had connections with this church in the 16th century and by his will directed his body to be buried here. The tomb is still there, covered by an alabaster slab, from which the brasses have long since disappeared no-one knows where.

Needless to say, the precious key was returned with alacrity.

Hyde Heath

On a 16th century map of the area, the village is shown as simply 'Hide' and the common opposite as 'Hide Heath'. In the interim, the spelling has changed and both village and common together are now called Hyde Heath and, with later development, it straddles a long, wooded ridge of the Chilterns. Few guide books even mention it, and those that do waste few words on it.

Many years ago the common was covered with gorse and scrub and, according to one writer, the footpath across it from Missenden afforded 'the most alluring route to Chesham.' Since then an arena of green has been cleared for the accommodation of childrens' amusements, a pavilion and a pitch for cricket battles in the summer. The Plough, across the road that runs along the edge of the common, provides celebration for winners and solace for losers.

The common is surrounded by woodland and small brick and flint cottages. The church of St Andrew, looking for all the world just like another cottage save for the cross on top, peeps from behind the school. In the church there is an altar painting of the Nativity painted by two local artists who used as models villagers past and present and local scenery. On the other side of the road is the small post office cum village shop that sells just about everything. Perhaps most things about Hyde Heath are on a small scale, but it has a community spirit as big as they come.

It was in 1825 that the Disraeli family came from town to this part of the Chilterns, renting Hyde House for the summer months – a large, white residence with a long, straight drive fronting on to the Chesham-Missenden road. Benjamin's father, Isaac, a well-known writer in the London literary world of his day, decided that this place on its high ridge would be a healthy spot for his family to enjoy pleasant breaks from unhealthy London and 'its hourly seductions'. Later he purchased the manor house at Bradenham as a permanent residence, but it was here at Hyde House that the young Benjamin Disraeli wrote his first novel, *Vivian Grey*. The future Prime Minister of England must have enjoyed the surrounding woods and fields and walking on the wild heath – or did he miss those 'hourly seductions'?

The earliest mention of a meeting of the Baptist Union at Hyde Heath is in the Spring Edition of the Oxford Journal of 1779 which describes an incident whereby some uncouth person tried to disrupt the meeting held in the cottage of Mr James Sleap. Mr Sleap, being of a forgiving nature, refused to prosecute. Later meetings were held in a small chapel 'down the common' which is now a house.

The present Union chapel, built of brick, was opened in 1932 and stands right next door to the village hall, which is perhaps the most unusual building in the village. It is an old Army Nissen Hut (Dining Hall) purchased from Halton Camp around 1924. Apparently, a stalwart, rather decorous lady resident of Hyde Heath became alarmed that in her opinion far too many men and women of the village were spending an inordinate amount of time in the pubs. So she managed to acquire the hut from Halton in order to provide them with another venue for amusement. And it worked! Ever since, this hall has been the scene of great activity in this small but vibrant community. During the Second World War it was the training centre for both the Red Cross and the Home Guard, with ammunition stored in biscuit tins in the kitchen. Today it is the very hub of village life with groups of people constantly hurrying and scurrying through its portals preparing for some forthcoming event – drama productions, playgroups, meetings, jumble sales etc. And Hyde Heath are not content with just one Women's Institute, they have two – morning and afternoon – and it was the WI who raised the funds for the village hall back in the 1920s.

Let's hope that no bright spark in the future suggests building another one – it would never be the same.

And talking of sparks – in 1931 little Hyde Heath received mention in the national press for holding the largest Guy Fawkes Bonfire in Buckinghamshire!

Ibstone

◥│The little church of St Nicholas is well and truly hidden, and a search is necessary, though walkers may stumble upon it by accident. It stands on a platform of green about a mile to the south of the village, which stretches along a ridge of the Chilterns some 700 ft above sea level and affords splendid views on either side of the Turville and Hambleden valleys.

The writer, Dame Rebecca West, loved it here and lived for many years in the manor house that stands near the school and green at the top of the leafy lane that leads down to the church. There is evidence that there were once cottages down this lane and that, for some reason they fell into decay, some say due to the Black Death, and they are now no more. Over the centuries the focal point of the village seems to have shifted further along the ridge towards the common, leaving the church some distance away.

As a result, some parishioners have a great distance to cover when attending service, and legend has it that at one time an attempt was made to build a new church in a more convenient spot, but the Devil got to hear of it and took a dislike to the proposed new site and, during the course of erection, removed the structure so many times, that the builders decided to abandon the idea. Not surprisingly, the spot is now called Hell Corner!

Taking the single track opposite the brick and flint school, the road dips away with still no sign of the church behind its leafy green screen until one is practically on top of it. At the gate stands a broken stone coffin that was discovered in a nearby field and in the churchyard is an ancient yew said to be 1,000 years old with a girth of some 16 feet. From here, the views to the Turville valley are superb with stretches of this heavenly countryside literally falling away to beech-woods and meadows of sheep and lambs. The 17th century Manor Farm is just a little way further down the hill.

The Normans built most of this church and it is of great architectural interest. Pevsner calls it 'picturesque and singular', and so it is. It is a squat building with a short timbered bellcote which makes the whole appear snub-nosed. Entry is from a wooden porch through a 12th century doorway and inside, it is a cool, peaceful sanctuary.

The 15th century carved oak pulpit is something to behold and may well have been one of the first in the country, as prior to this it was usual to preach from the steps of the chancel. The priest who used it first could not have wholly trusted his parishioners as there is a staple to which the bible was chained. But at least sermons cannot have gone on too long as there is also a small support for an hour glass.

Standing in this small church from which village and habitation seems divorced, the true meaning of solitary contemplation and repose is realised. Until the breeze rustles through the trees outside and the old church door creaks . . .

Ickford

The river Thame that streams past this village forms the county boundary line with Oxfordshire and down here, about half a mile from the church, it is spanned by a long, four-arched bridge. One arch is of brick and the others of stone and almost dead centre is a double plaque which reads on one side:

'1685. The County of Oxon ends here.'

and on the other

'The County of Bucks begins here.'

But there has been a bridge here since 1237 and long before that it is thought to have been the site where Edward the Elder made a treaty with the Danes in AD 906. It certainly is a peaceful spot among buttercupped water meadows, with willows and cattle standing along the banks of the gentle, flowing river.

The annual Tug of War takes place here between the brawn of the village of Tiddington, just over the border in Oxfordshire, and that of Ickford in Buckinghamshire, each team endeavouring, amid grunts, groans and heaves from the participants and shouts of encouragement from onlookers, to pull the other across the river into their county. Invariably one team or the other, or both, end up in the Thame.

Tug of War is not the only game the people of Ickford have

enjoyed over the centuries. Cut into the stone window sill in a side window of the north aisle of the church is a rough marking-out for the ancient game of Nine Men's Morris, a board game something like chess that could be played on any flat surface. It was often marked out, sometimes in church porches or any convenient spot where the players felt like a game, even in the turf of village greens. Shakespeare mentions it in *A Midsummer Night's Dream* when he has Titania say, presumably after a shower, 'The Nine Men's Morris is filled up with mud.'

Relics of this game are now exceedingly rare, although one marking is said to exist on a tomb at Dunster in Somerset, and another at Finchingfield, Essex. The board, or marking-out, had 24 stations, and counters could either be coloured pegs or pebbles. Each player started out with nine of these 'men', hence the title of the game, and the object was to arrange them in lines of three, whilst preventing your opponent from doing the same. Each time you were successful, you could take a man from the other side. The way to win was either to get all the opposing men off the board or to corner your opponent. The window sill is high at Ickford and any two players of long ago would have had to stand.

Whilst visiting this attractive church of St Nicholas with its Norman tower and saddleback roof, it would be a pity to miss the remarkable memorial that a certain Thomas Tipping had erected to himself in 1595, a few years before he died, presumably to ensure that the sentiments he had in mind were correctly expressed to posterity. The monument also includes 'his chaste wife' and nine children, four sons and five daughters. He and his wife appear within black marble columns and the nine children, segregated and in varying sizes, kneel beneath in cute humility, each with the initial of their Christian name over their respective heads. There also appear other little heads clad in strange Red Indian head-dresses.

Rector of Ickford in the 17th century and living at the rectory nearby was Gilbert Sheldon, largely remembered for the Sheldonian Theatre at Oxford which was built in 1699. Being a friend and adviser to Charles I, he was active in those troubles that led up to the Civil War and was markedly anti-Puritan. He was rewarded for his loyalty after the Restoration by Charles II and was made Archbishop of Canterbury in 1663. He was rector of this delightful village from 1636 to 1660.

The personality of Canon Vernon Staley is definitely imprinted on this little church. He was rector here from 1911 to 1933 and was an outstanding carver in wood. In his workshop at the rectory he made the elaborate font cover which is lifted by a pulley. He also made the tester above the altar, candlesticks, altar rails, lectern and benches, and gave the church the Royal Arms of King George V that adorns the front of the gallery. These arms were coloured by his son, Edward Staley, during his last leave before returning to the Front where he was killed in the First World War. The Canon's love for his son also pervades the church in the stained glass window to his memory depicting Edward I and Edward the Martyr by Sir Ninian Comper, the distinguished church architect and designer.

It was by lucky accident that I stumbled upon the sibling hamlet of Little Ickford and was entranced by the 16th, 17th and 18th century picturesque houses and cottages and their gardens full of colour and fragrance.

Ilmer

The mother duck emerged from the pond and walked sedately across the close-cropped green, closely followed by at least a dozen ducklings that could not have been more than two or three days old. They walked in column of twos with such precision that one could almost hear the tap of a kettle drum. Mother knew exactly where she was going when she crossed the lane, turned into the farm gate, and disappeared, the last little offspring throwing a glance towards us as he performed a slick exit stage right.

Such is the peace of this small hamlet that lies at the end of a lane off the Thame-Princes Risborough road, that Mother Duck had nothing to fear – there was no-one about, not a

Cottage at Ilmer

sign of a cat, or even the bark of a dog. In the low-lying country near the Oxfordshire border, there are plenty of ponds and water meadows and birds are rife. Mallards glide across the surface of a pond through garlands of overhanging willow, and further up the lane, a moorhen, feeding her only pampered chick, who was by no means handsome, did not feel inclined to move out of our way.

The Norman possessor of this manor in the 11th century was Odo, Bishop of Bayeaux, and the tenure was held on condition that its owner was Marshall of the King's Hawks and Falcons, a contract that continued for several centuries. This fact is only mentioned in lowered tones when ducks are present.

There is just a handful of picturesque cottages, some timbered and thatched. Under a chestnut tree on the borders of one flourished a clump of edelweiss, the garden of another was full of wallflowers, and the heavenly church of St Peter had a thriving honeysuckle twining around the gate.

The church is built of stone with weatherboarded bell-turret and remarkable pyramidal roof and spire. On entering the small interior, the view of the chancel is framed and enhanced by the beautiful carved wooden rood screen that stands on a low stone wall and is thought to be 15th century or possibly earlier. A line of roses ornaments the wooden cornice above the tracery. The octagonal font is possibly 14th century with a 17th century oak cover.

High up on the wall of the nave are carvings of two angels with wings outspread in full flight, whilst two others stand guard over the door, left wing down, right wing up, as if giving hand signals. The shimmering bright colours from a window depicting the Good Samaritan catch the eye and on the north window of the chancel are two unusual carvings depicting the Trinity and St Christopher.

Ilmer is known for its independent little community, for the church was restored in 1860 largely from the pocket of the Reverend Partridge, the incumbent of the time and, in the late 1960s, the people of this tiny place themselves organised events and raised enough funds to pay for restoration and redecoration works. And they did it once again in 1978 when an appeal was launched for funds to smarten up the spire and tower and restore the bells. Most of the work was completed the following year.

Ivinghoe

'Tring, Wing and Ivinghoe,
Hampden of Hampden did forego,
For striking the Black Prince a blow,
And glad he was to escape so.'

This is another of those Buckinghamshire rhymes that last for centuries and there are a variety of versions. This one is supposed to refer to the legend that one of John Hampden's ancestors in a fit of pique during a game of tennis went so far as to strike the Black Prince a blow and, as a result, he lost three manors. Some say the game was checkers, but in any event, it is considered a wild story as no Hampden at any time owned Tring, Wing or Ivinghoe.

Sir Walter Scott, the novelist, heard this jingle whilst visiting Ivinghoe during the early part of the 19th century, and took the title for his novel and its hero from the name of the village, but he spelt it wrongly and it turned out 'Ivanhoe'. The rhyme has such a lovely lilt that the local people just could not resist playing around and we have 'Tring, Wing and Ivinghoe, three steeples in a row' to name just one of the many variations handed down for generations.

Ivinghoe is now a village with a large green, but it was not always so. It was once a town of size, supporting a market, fair and court-house, now the quaintly gabled Parish Room. It is easy to see why it was a place of importance. Standing as it does at the edge of the Chiltern Hills and at the junction of the ancient Upper and Lower Icknield Ways, it was on the road for wayfarers travelling through the Tring gap to the north-west. It is surrounded by delightful countryside and stands out against a backcloth of hills that are mostly owned by the National Trust. Beacon Hill at over 760 ft is the most dominant.

It is the fine, cruciform church of St Mary that dominates the village and by its size alone reveals Ivinghoe's imposing past. Edward the Confessor granted the manor to the See of Winchester and it remained in the possession of the Bishops of Winchester until 1551. The rambling old King's Head Inn, together with some old houses, stands opposite the church and on the churchyard wall there hangs suspended an iron hook on the end of a huge wooden shaft bound with iron. This is so large it could barely be supported by three men and was used in an emergency to pull thatch or timber from the roof of a burning cottage. Underneath is an example of the most commonly used deterrent to trespassers – a man-trap.

On entering the church an unusual impact is received

from 38 poppyheads (carved ends of benches or pews) that date from the 15th century. The medieval craftsmen really let themselves go and carved faces of fantasy cunningly and cleverly concealed in the wood. Little faces, or even parts of faces – a leering smile here, puckered lips there – perhaps on one an impish gnome and on another a snarling dragon – all with individual expressions. In most cases the natural end of the poppyhead has been used either to form swirling hair or a hat. Look for the one on the last but one pew opposite the south door and you will find a mermaid. The whole gives the effect that a goblin congregation awaits your coming, and each one is guaranteed to intrigue.

The wooden roof is supported by angels with outspread wings and is mid 15th century. There are carved wooden figures of apostles at the end of the beams and beneath them are stone corbels with grinning heads.

The richly carved pulpit is Jacobean with a sounding board or tester and back panel relief of the Resurrection, which is thought to have been damaged during the Civil War.

Lying in a recess on the north side of the chancel is the defaced stone figure of a priest, whose identity has caused much speculation. The local people had no trouble and in the past called him 'Grandfather Greybeard'.

When leaving this truly remarkable church, one is confronted by a wooden notice dated 1875 which announces that a grant had been received towards reseating the church in such a way as to provide additional accommodation and going on to say that the sittings were all free, subject to allotment by the churchwardens. But most touching is the last line – 'Suitable provisions will be made for the poorer inhabitants.'

Jordans

People travel from the four corners of the earth to visit Jordans with its group of historic buildings – and it is well worth it. For here is the early 17th century farmhouse of Old Jordans where those fearless Quakers held their meetings despite great persecution, often raided and dragged off to prison. It is now a Guest House and Conference Centre, but one can still imagine those Friends of yesteryear walking to the meeting through the leafy lanes and meadows in their broadbrimmed hats and modest clothes. It was here they met before the little Meeting House, brick with hipped roof, was built further down the lane in 1688, just prior to the passing of the Toleration Act which permitted such buildings to be erected. Americans especially come to pay their respects to the grave of William Penn, founder of Pennsylvania, who lies buried in a peaceful green glade in front of the Meeting House in the company of those enduring friends he knew – Isaac Penington, Thomas Ellwood and their families; all dauntless Quakers in this part of the country.

Between these two buildings stands the great black barn built of timbers said to be from the *Mayflower*. This capacious building is used today for all manner of functions such as concerts, dramatic productions by the Jordans Players and popular booksales etc.

But how many of these visitors think to take the lane almost opposite these buildings – Seer Green Lane – to the comparatively modern village of Jordans with its attractive red brick gabled houses clustered around a green where cricket is played in summer. Some of the houses are in roads off and there is a purpose built village shop, school and hall.

The building of this village in 1919 was yet another example of the foresight, determination and persistence shown by the Society of Friends and somehow a worthy continuation of their remarkable history connected with Jordans. It was in 1916 that the Friends were horrified to hear that Dean Farm with 102 acres of land, some of which lay directly opposite the Meeting House, was up for sale and that developers were avidly interested in building housing estates there. The peace that was the very essence of Jordans was threatened and stood to be destroyed for ever. There was only one alternative. Beat the developers at their own game and buy the property themselves. This way they could preserve the land around Jordans itself and build their own village just out of sight over the ridge.

By 1918 the purchase was completed and Fred Rowntree presented his plans for the layout of the village to the local council for approval. Building started in 1919, commemorative bricks being ceremonially laid on the 15th February of that year.

The following summer, at the north end of the village, clay for brickmaking was discovered and the village industries produced their own bricks for the building, which were of excellent quality. Jordans Village Ltd came into being with its own Management Committee dealing with administration and maintenance. Excitement plus a certain blend of the old freedom-loving, pioneering spirit of their forefathers was in the air. The village was intended to create a community based on Christian principles, though it was not necessary to be a Quaker to live there.

Work progressed and by 1920 there were 65 people living in the new village. They had won, they thought. They had done what they set out to do – preserve the quiet of Jordans for ever – when, in 1928, their peace of mind was rudely shattered.

The local council announced that they proposed to build an arterial road that would carry busy traffic right by Jordans. Not only people of the area and county protested, but from all over the British Isles came letters of strong objection and many, some famous, wrote in shocked terms to such national newspapers as *The Times* and *Spectator*. Questions were even raised in the House, and the little council eventually shrank back into its offices, all plans for the road abandoned forever.

Today there are approximately 400 people living in the village and the houses have a well-established look. Furthermore, they have their own Councillor representing them on the Chalfont St Giles Parish Council – and so the peace and sheer enchantment of the little Buckinghamshire hollow that is Jordans remains for all to sample.

Latimer

➤ During the South African War, at the Battle of Boshof on 5th April 1900, two distinguished noblemen – one French, one British – both with vast military experience, faced one another across the battlefield.

General Count de Villebois Mareuil had fought with honour in the Franco-Prussian War of 1870 and had become quite famous as an officer and writer on the merits of the life of a professional soldier. He had resigned as Commander of the French Foreign Legion in order to offer his valuable services to the Boers in the war against the British. The Boers had put him in charge of all foreign troops, volunteers from many other European countries.

On the other side stood Charles Compton William Cavendish, third Baron Chesham of Latimer House in the far away county of Buckinghamshire. He too had served his country with distinction in both the Coldstream Guards and Tenth Hussars in India. Upon his retirement in 1879, he had joined the Royal Bucks Hussars and ten years later became their Colonel.

After 'Black Week', as it was called, during the South African War, when the British had suffered such a series of defeats at the hands of the Boers that the public became seriously alarmed, a dismayed War Cabinet met. From this came a request to Lord Chesham to organise an entirely new force of Imperial Yeomanry, which he did. Then, in command of the Tenth Battalion, which contained two Buckinghamshire companies, he had set out for South Africa in January 1900, where he was given command of the whole Yeomanry Brigade.

Now these two soldiers with similar lives and careers faced one another in battle. The Boers were ensconced on a hill and were much the stronger force. Nothing daunted, Lord Chesham gave the order to attack and his men advanced swiftly up the slope. There was a sharp engagement and it was not long before it became apparent that the British were winning the day. Nevertheless, de Villebois fought bravely, urging his men on, when a shell struck him in the head and he fell dead from his horse.

The British were the victors, and the men cheered and hurrahed loudly, but Lord Chesham stood sadly over the body of his worthy adversary. He gave orders that the body of de Villebois be buried there with full military honours and a stone erected to mark the grave. His wounded horse was later brought back to Buckinghamshire by Lord Chesham, who named him *Villebois* after his master.

Villebois spent eleven happy years grazing peacefully in lovely Latimer Park alongside the river Chess and when he died, Lord Chesham had his heart and trappings buried in the middle of the pretty village green right next to the memorial to the 100 men from the surrounding villages who died in that South African War. A stone marks the grave of the horse and the memorial tells the story of those brave men of long ago.

On Coombe Hill, a prominent point in the Chilterns, there stands a monument to all the men of Buckinghamshire who fell in the Boer War and at the bottom of the Market Square at Aylesbury there is a very impressive statue of Charles Compton William Cavendish, third Baron Chesham.

The Lee

➤ Many people driving along the road from The Barley Mow at the top of Frith Hill, Great Missenden to the village of The Lee and pastures beyond, have received a very nasty shock, especially at night. For suddenly, looking over a hedge directly in front of them, appears a huge, glaring face of florid hue, with piercing eyes and lips pursed in anger. If and when one can pluck up enough courage to proceed along the road, it is soon discovered to be (of all things) a ship's figurehead, carved out of solid oak and weighing two tons. It came from the last wooden warship to be built in the British Navy and was called *The Howe*, later to be known as *HMS Impregnable*. What's more, the face on the figurehead is that of Admiral Earl Howe himself, who was in charge of the

Channel Fleet during the French Revolutionary Wars. Under his leadership, they attacked a convoy escorted by French warships carrying corn to France from the United States. It was some miles west of Ushant where the skirmish took place and, on the 'Glorious First of June' 1794 the British captured six enemy ships and sunk another. It was considered a great Naval victory, so why he should look so angry is something of a mystery.

The ship was not broken up until the 1920s when it was offered for sale and purchased by the Liberty family, mainly for its timbers which were used in the reconstruction of the famous Liberty Store in Regent Street, London. The founder of the emporium was Sir Arthur Liberty, a haberdasher from Chesham, who later became the lord of the manor of The Lee.

No-one can visit the quaint village of The Lee with the pile of sarsen stones on its green surrounded by cottages and a pub, without also visiting the two churches.

The Lee Old Church

At the lychgate to the churchyard are clusters of erica and primroses and one is immediately confronted by the new church built in the 1860s of red brick. It seems a surprisingly extensive, well-used churchyard for so small a village, and tucked away behind the church is an absolute jewel. The Lee Old Church was built of chalk and clay (clunch) in the 12th century and was once a chapel of ease. The east window contains a small piece of 13th century glass and also depicts the three great champions of freedom of 17th century England – Hampden, Hobart and Cromwell. At the beginning of this century this window was offered to the church at Great Hampden, only a few miles away and where John Hampden lies buried, but amazingly the gift was refused due, it was said, to the fact that it contained a portrait of Cromwell. A long time to bear a grudge, it would seem.

Lillingstone Dayrell

Lillingstone Dayrell was once part of the forest of Whittlewood and lies close to Stowe School Park and the county border. It is to the east of the main road from Buckingham to Northampton and derives its name from the family of Dayrell who were established here as far back as Saxon times. They turned out to be one of those families whose estates passed down to generation after generation for century after century and their pedigree takes up two whole pages in Lipscombe's County History.

Many of their memorials are to be seen in the 11th century church of St Nicholas, which has some interesting 13th century tiles. Perhaps the most impressive is the free standing tomb chest to Paul and Dorothy Dayrell (1571) which supports their reclining figures. Their features are very finely sculptured. He is clad in armour with his feet resting on a lion, whilst Dorothy is in a finely embroidered dress with puffed sleeves and has a goat's head at her feet. Their sons and daughters kneel in salutation.

The Dayrells were never afraid of public office and served

the county in many official capacities, but for bravery perhaps it is Walter Haddon (1516–71), also born in Lillingstone Dayrell, who gained most admiration. He lived at the same time as Paul and Dorothy Dayrell and, though not part of a glittering family, he did very well for himself, by ordinary standards and became an Eton scholar. He always averred that his learning and success was wholly due to the efforts of his mother on his behalf. He became a well-known statesman and writer at the court of the great Queen Elizabeth and also served Her Majesty as Ambassador at Bruges and elsewhere.

Then came the rub – the Queen made him her Master of Requests, which was considered one of the most onerous jobs at court. Walter was expected to chase an extremely reluctant Queen with petitions which required her attention. She was seldom in the mood, if ever, and, if she could, would avoid Walter like the plague. He in turn became completely fed up trying to catch her attention.

The Queen was so annoyed when one day he made it into her presence that she called out to him in irritation 'Fie, sloven, thy new boots stink!' Whereupon Walter, just as exasperated, sharply replied: 'Madam! It is not my boots which stink, but the old stale petitions that have been so long in my bag unopened!' Good for Walter!

Little Hampden

➤ Aunt Lene had been born Selina Porter of Little Kimble. She had married around 1880 and went to live with her husband in the cottage tucked up against the church at Little Hampden, a small hamlet set deep in the beechwoods, reached only by the winding uphill lane leading to nowhere along one of the ridges of the Chilterns and ending in a mere track at The Rising Sun.

She received the cottage rent free in return for looking after the church and here, in this small abode, she gave birth at regular intervals to a total of twelve children, losing the first two in a smallpox epidemic which swept through the nine families that made up the hamlet.

Aunt Lene loved the church – one of the smallest in the county, it seats only 35 people. She kept it as clean as a new pin, sweeping and polishing its brasses and silver until they gleamed in the light of the lancet windows. Built originally of flint and rubble, but restored with brick covered with plaster, the primitive looking 15th century porch is intriguing and has two storeys, the top one serving as a belfry. The pointed arch of the doorway is formed by the natural line of two great rough weathered oak trunks.

Most important are the wall paintings that were discovered in 1907 and are believed to date from the reign of Henry III.

It was thought at one time that a picture or effigy of St Christopher on the walls of the church gave immunity from sudden death to those who feasted their eyes upon it. Whether it worked for anyone in Little Hampden will probably never be known, but two of the wall paintings are of this saint, one of which is said to be among the oldest in England.

Life was not easy for Aunt Lene washing and cooking for a family of ten, yet it was to her that the rest of the village turned for advice and in times of trouble. She was always ready with her characteristic warmth and quick sympathy, not to mention practical help. She visited anyone who was ill and comforted those who were laid low. Night and morning in all seasons she set off with her lantern, a candle burning inside, to Hampden Common to put two old ladies to bed who could not make it themselves and returned in the morning to get them up.

Her cooking was renowned, especially her Bucks Clanger which hung simmering in a pot over the grate from early morning. This unrivalled county dish consists of pieces of bacon, potatoes, onions and parsley, all wrapped up in a suet blanket. A grocer rattled up the lane occasionally, but regularly once a week in all weathers Aunt Lene in her long skirt walked the three miles to Great Missenden to shop and trudged the three miles back. Her children walked daily the two and a half miles to Prestwood school and back – then queued for the cottage toilet at the top of the long garden.

To ensure that her family always had enough and the best of food, Aunt Lene worked long in her garden, growing vegetables and fruit until it was near to bursting with a rich harvest. The fuel for the copper and the winter fires she gathered from the extensive Hampden Woods.

A true countrywoman, never did that lovely, benign face lose its serenity, perhaps something reflected from her little church, and she was much too busy thinking of others to complain or bemoan her lot.

She died in 1926 and the hamlet mourned her. Continuing the St Christopher theme, they placed a charming lancet window in the chancel in her name, dedicating it to one 'ever ready to bear another's burdens'. Here St Christopher appears in the most heavenly shade of blue robe, carrying the Child.

Aunt Lene would have been pleased to know that her son, George, carried on tending the church after her death, lavishing upon it the same loving care his mother had bestowed. Although he had lost his sight, he kept the churchyard neat and tidy, trimming the hedges to immaculate proportions he could not see.

Authur Mee calls the church 'an astonishing little treasury to find by a crooked lane in the heart of quiet country' and between them, mother and son cared for it for very nearly a century.

Little Kimble

They lived in Brookside House in the middle of the last century – Charles and Nancy Porter and their family of three girls and four boys. It was a large, airy house in which to spend a childhood, set in the heart of the Chilterns with the Bonny Brook running by, and the apple tree in the garden bearing enough fruit to pay the rent.

The population of the village was so small that the diminutive church of All Saints could accommodate the whole with comfort. It stood only a quarter of a mile from Great Kimble church where John Hampden, with others, had made his stand and refused to pay the Ship Money levied against him by Charles I without the authority of Parliament. In that church there is today a facsimile reproduction of the official record showing the signatures of Hampden and the other freeholders.

In response to the call from the two jolly green bells that danced and swung in the bellcote, the Porter family regularly attended Little Kimble church with their neighbours and every Sunday in their best clothes they walked up the path with precision and in column of twos. Sitting in the ancient atmosphere, they enjoyed the services and particularly the music.

All Saints is a treasure of a church and is still untouched by the centuries and is practically hidden from the Princes Risborough – Aylesbury Road, save for that saucy little bellcote. Inside, the 14th century wall paintings have been described by expert Clive Rouse as 'artistically the best in Bucks'. Particularly beautiful is the rare representation of St Francis preaching to the birds in a tree. There are also some intriguing 13th century tiles showing subjects from the Arthurian romances, and fragments of medieval glass with the arms of France and England.

The village to this day is not large, although in the early part of this century a little railway arrived with a track running from Aylesbury to Princes Risborough. The small station has now been made into a pretty dwelling, but trains still run through.

At the early age of five, the Porter girls were sent to the village lace school – just a large room in a cottage. Here they were taught discipline and control, how to persevere with the bobbins and pins, and how to write their names.

There were exciting times when the villagers grouped together for celebrations and the family Sunday walks to Velvet Lawn. And the time when the old lady was advised to place her money in the Bank in case of fire in her cottage. The only bank she knew was the warren and she placed her life savings deep inside one of the countless rabbit holes without marking it. Later she became frantic when she failed to remember which one. The whole village declared a holiday and, armed with shovels and spades, they spent the whole of the next day at the warren looking for the treasure. The sun was setting when a weary shout went up – 'Found!' Now that's community spirit!

Little Marlow

The tubs of scarlet geraniums standing outside the porch of the church of St John the Baptist provided a splash of colour against the green background. Although portions of this church are 12th century, there have been a variety of additions throughout the centuries. It stands, together with the pretty group of Mansion House, inn and red brick cottages at the end of a cul-de-sac off the A4155, about half a mile from the river Thames.

Adjoining Abbey Farm there once stood the Benedictine nunnery of St Mary de Fontibus, which was there in the 13th century. It was always reputed to be rather small and at the Dissolution of the Monasteries it was reported that there were only two nuns and four servants living there.

Along the A4155 towards Bourne End is the sign for 'Little Marlow Cemetery'. Here is the memorial of the great man who had such associations with the county, loved it so well and lived at nearby Bourne End.

Born in 1875 at Greenwich of poor beginnings, Edgar Wallace was educated at London elementary schools. As soon as he was of age, he joined the army and served in South Africa where he managed to achieve his first writing job as war correspondent. On his return to this country, he became a fully fledged journalist, but in his spare time he wrote the first of his exciting novels. Success came with the publication of *The Four Just Men* and *Sanders of the River*. He continued to write and by the 1920s he was acknowledged as one of the most prolific and popular writers ever, also writing plays and numerous newspaper and magazine articles, and his earnings became colossal. He was however extremely extravagant, particulary where race horses were concerned.

By now he had become interested in films, especially those of his own stories, and he actually founded the Beaconsfield Film Studios. He fell in love with this part of the country and purchased his house at Bourne End. With the coming of the 'talkies', he set about directing the film of one of his own novels, *The Squeaker*.

Although his work in films alone would be enough to daunt most people, there was absolutely no reduction in his writings and at the same time he took an interest in local affairs, which is probably why he was approached by the Liberal Agent for the Aylesbury Division of Bucks to become a parliamentary Liberal candidate. The idea attracted him and, in order to further his political ambitions, he founded the *Bucks Mail*, a weekly journal, written mostly by himself. It goes without saying that he was a brilliant orator and people remember to this day his charismatic personality when he spoke at various political rallies.

But something went wrong, and it became plain that he was fighting a losing battle, perhaps due to his extravagance and addiction to gambling. He withdrew from politics and in 1931 accepted an invitation to go to Hollywood. There he died in 1932 and when his body was returned to England, the whole nation mourned, flags flew at half-mast at Southampton, and the Fleet Street churchbells tolled. He ended his journey in the countryside he loved, near the river Thames, and in peaceful Little Marlow.

Little Missenden

Little Missenden is more than happy to lie unnoticed in a niche of the Chilterns just off the busy A413. It is a charming place, backed by beechwoods, the little river Misbourne flowing through the meadows and cottages clustering around an ancient church, manor house and two pubs, the Red Lion and the Crown. The landlords of these two hostelries are brothers – Ron and Alan Howe, born in the village, and sons of a local farmer.

'One of the most ideal spots on this island' wrote a guest from Canada in the visitors' book of the Red Lion during the early part of this century. This book is a delight and was kept by an aunt of the Howe brothers when she was landlady before the First World War. The village was well and truly off the beaten track in those days and most visitors seem to have stumbled upon it by lucky accident. The teas served are described in the language of the day as 'capital', 'famous', and 'ripping'.

The quaint 12th century church of St John the Baptist looks unpretentious from the outside, but its 12th and 13th century wall paintings, which were not discovered until 1931, have been described by the experts as 'remarkable' and 'astonishing'. There are quite a few to look at; in particular the one of St Christopher carrying the Christchild over the river is a striking sight as you enter the building. The saint stands 10 ft high and, in the rippling water around his feet, swim an eel and a pike.

The manor house is a pleasant, mellow, Jacobean building where lived Dr Benjamin Bates (1730–1828), who was personal physician to Sir Francis Dashwood, the founder of the notorious Hell Fire Club. Dr Bates was also a member himself, visiting Medmenham and West Wycombe frequently, but he always denied that any untoward practices took place, save perhaps for a certain amount of excessive drinking. Be that as it may, whatever went on it seems to have brought him little physical harm as he lived to the ripe old age of 98.

Dr Bates had a passionate interest in art and was a friend and patron to many artists. He visited Rome in the company of the renowned sculptor, John Flaxman. The great Sir Joshua Reynolds, first President of the Royal Academy, thought nothing of slipping down to his old friend at the manor house for the occasional weekend in the company of his lady friend, Angelica Kauffman, a Swiss artist of some repute. Whilst she was there, enjoying the peace of the countryside, she designed the charming terrace and garden at the rear, making good use of the waters of the Misbourne.

Dr Bates left a valuable collection of pictures which were removed to Stowe after his death, he having willed them to the Duke of Buckingham.

Not only did Little Missenden have connections with the world of art, but also literature and journalism. John Dunton (1659–1773), one of the early printers of newspapers, was born here. As a young lad he was apprenticed to a London bookseller, and eventually set up on his own in the trade, and became very successful. The news-sheet he published was *Athenian Mercury*, a single leaf which cost one penny, but later he transformed it into a quarterly magazine. He was said to have rather eccentric habits and was considered by some to be downright 'peculiar'. In fact, Isaac Disraeli, the father of Benjamin, described him as 'that cracked brain bookseller'. He had financial difficulties and ended up in the Fleet for debt. The last we hear of the unfortunate Mr Dunton is when he issued from that place *Dying Groans from the Fleet Prison*.

Marlow

It is well known that gout is an extremely painful condition, and that sudden movement or unexpected knocks can send the patient into a fit nearing apoplexy and a frame of mind murderous to any other human being within sight. If any family were only too fully aware of the sufferings and deprivations of this malady, it was the Cecil family of Hatfield House in Hertfordshire. They were martyrs to it and found it necessary every so often to journey to Bath to partake of the beneficial waters.

But the journey was sheer torture. It was not only long and arduous but the roads were in a shocking condition. Badly in need of repair, filled with ruts, boulders and un-trimmed hedges and trees, one can easily imagine the ago-nies of the gouty passenger bouncing up and down in the narrow confines of a carriage, desperately trying to shield the heavily swathed foot or toe, perhaps by sticking it out of the window. The cries and wails wafting up to the driver must have been a great burden to bear.

The family, therefore, decided to take measures to shorten the journey. They developed a short cut through to Marlow, thereby cutting out London, and joining the Bath Road at Reading. This route went by way of Watford, Rickmansworth, Amersham, Hazlemere, High Wycombe, Marlow and Henley and, for obvious reasons, became known as 'the Gout Track'.

In the early 18th century, most roads were the responsibility of the parish, who were charged and expected to keep them in good condition. This was, to say the least, an onerous burden, for contributions were negligible and the money was not easily forthcoming – so that the roads were either repaired in a cheap, haphazard way, or not at all.

The only answer to this was to set up a toll road, along which there would be turnpikes where people would be expected to pay a fee to go over a certain stretch of road and thereby contribute to a much improved upkeep. A body of Turnpike Trustees was usually created by landowners (like the Cecils), and farmers or local merchants whose business interests were furthered by better roads. At the instigation of the afflicted family, the Hatfield to Reading Turnpike Trust was set up and there were many toll houses or turnpikes that lined the route, one at the Queen's Head at Amersham, another at Hazlemere and others at Wycombe Hill, Marlow and Henley.

There were also milestones, and the one in the Market Place at Marlow, which forms the 36th in the chain marking the 'Gout Track' from Hatfield to Reading, is the most impressive of them all. It is a four-sided obelisk of stone which bears the inscription:

'Wycombe 5, Aylesbury 22, Oxford by Stokenchurch 25, Hatfield 36. Erected by the Trustees of the Reading and Hatfield Road. September 1822.'

These toll roads were not always popular with the people, despite the better conditions. They sometimes objected to some of the payments demanded and to the length of time they often had to stand in line at the turnpike. But they could be lucrative and the accounts of the Hatfield to Reading Turnpike Trust show an annual revenue of £2,000 between the years 1822 and 1843.

In the whole of the country, 22,000 miles of road had been turnpiked by 1838, but from 1888 County Councils had assumed responsibility for main roads, and by 1890 there were only two Turnpike Trusts left. But in Buckinghamshire we still have reminders of the old 'Gout Track' with signs now and then along its route directing either to Bath or Hatfield.

Marsh Gibbon

Friendly Societies were started in the 17th century and were a form of mutual insurance against sickness and old age, and by the 18th century their numbers had increased considerably, not only in Buckinghamshire but all over the country. Inadequacy in contributions and lack of any kind of legal standing shortened the lives of many, but the first Friendly Society Acts of 1793 and 1795 afforded some kind of recognition, protection and encouragement and the movement grew. But long before this, in the year 1788 in the village of Marsh Gibbon close to the Oxfordshire border, the Greyhound Club had already been formed by bell ringers. In 1988 it celebrated its bi-centenary.

The Club derives its name from the picturesque Greyhound Inn in the village, which was described in 1700 as being tenanted by the Widow Rollings, an interesting character. The Club had a room on the first floor; today it meets in an outbuilding.

Rules were drawn up with regard to 'benefit from the Box' in the event of sickness or death and subscriptions were payable monthly.

Oakapple Day (29th May) was the birthday of Charles II and in 1664 it was commanded that the day should be observed as one of thanksgiving. In fact, there was a special

The Manor House at Marsh Gibbon

service in the book of Common Prayer for this day which was only expunged in 1859. The Club decided that their first Club Feast Day should be on Oakapple Day and it has been held on that day or the nearest Saturday to it ever since.

There are meetings on four quarter nights. On the one in May, the Marsh Gibbon Band plays and marches from the Plough to the Greyhound where the committee provides bread, cheese and beer and collects subscriptions. The Club Feast Day on Oakapple Day begins at 6 am with a potato peeling session in the village hall and a barrel of beer is tapped. After a roll call, led by the Band, and carrying the two Club flags, members march to the church for a service. Then back to the village hall for the Festival Lunch after which comes the appointment of officers. This is conducted in a fairly unorthodox manner, the Secretary announcing to the gathering at large 'You want a Secretary', whereupon with luck the reply comes back 'We've got one'. This marvellous day ends to the strains of the Band, which plays around the village during the afternoon and evening.

Obviously everyone in Marsh Gibbon enjoys the Club and is rightfully proud of it. There are not many of these colourful customs still in force after 200 years.

The village of Marsh Gibbon itself is picturesque with a 13th century church and can be traced back to Edward the Confessor when it was called Merse, the name Gibbon being derived from a family holding lands there at the time of King John. It is the lovely old Tudor manor house that catches the eye. Built of stone with high gables, it is a delightful sight and one of the remaining fine old manor houses in the county.

Lipscombe calls it the old manor house of the Crokes and adds that, after the death of Alexander Croke around 1757, it was converted into a farmhouse. Still in one of the rooms is the hatchment of Croke and Blount and it is said that should it ever leave the house, something of an unpleasant nature will befall the owner.

Mursley

In the second half of the 16th century, Sir John Fortescue was doing very nicely. Cousin and former tutor to Queen Elizabeth I, Chancellor of the Exchequer and MP for Buckinghamshire, he cut a considerable figure in the Government. He also had some weighty friends in Burleigh and Bacon, not to mention Raleigh and Essex, and had received rich rewards in money and land. In 1570 he became possessed of the manor of Salden, a small hamlet close to Mursley. Here he commenced to build a mansion of size which cost him £33,000, a lot of money for those days. By 1590 it was just about completed and was one of the finest country houses in all England. It was of 'excellent masonry in brick and stonework' with fronts 175 ft in length, a balustrade at the top, and nine gables with coats of arms decorating the windows. There were terraced gardens, a bowling green, and a lake that supplied the household with fish, whilst a windmill ground the corn. In all the house maintained 60 servants.

Sir John was in a position to entertain lavishly and it was not long before an inquisitive Queen was herself proposing a Royal Pilgrimage 'to Sir John Fortescue's in Buckinghamshire'. Her arrival must have caused great excitement in the market town of Mursley. Lying as it does half-way between Buckingham and Dunstable, it enjoyed some status and had supported weekly markets plus a three-day Annual Fair since the 13th century. Mursley's prosperity was helped along even further by the Fortescue's great wealth and stature. Sir John by this time was heavily involved in local affairs and had also acquired the manor of Mursley.

In 1603 James I and his wife and children were entertained at Salden House and a glittering display of the elite passed through Mursley when on 28th June some 22 gentlemen were dubbed knights.

When Sir John died in 1607, happily not departing in the same way as his father, Sir Adrian, who had lost his head on the block under Henry VIII, his son, Francis, succeeded him. The last of the Fortescues died in 1729, the line became extinct and eventually this great mansion was demolished.

With the passing of the Fortescues, the importance of Mursley as a town gradually declined. Fairs and markets were no longer held, the population dropped and today it is a small attractive village with many thatched cottages. All that is left of the magnificent Salden House is now part of Salden Farm, down a small road opposite the church.

There are some fine memorials to the Fortescues in the 13th century St Mary's church at Mursley, one to that first Sir John and his wife, who are kneeling. He is handsome and dashing in armour of black and gold and wears a red rose. There is also one to his son, Sir Francis and his wife, who are also depicted in a kneeling position. Very charming underneath are their ten children, six boys in red and four girls in blue.

In the last century, Thomas Beecham, the well-known manufacturer of the pills that became a household name, came to live at Mursley Hall. Apparently he was an eccentric character to say the least and it is somewhat surprising to think that Sir Thomas Beecham, the famous conductor, was his grandson.

Naphill

➤ It has been said that Stewkley is the longest village in the county, but Naphill must surely run it a close second. Once a mere clearing in the woods, its single main street is made up of old and new houses on either side and runs seemingly unendingly along a ridge of the Chilterns to the common, once a stop for drovers. Amid nearby woods are two circular earthworks. These indicate the pens where sheep and cattle were kept to graze overnight. Here also, marked by a portuguese laurel, are the remains of a drover's Inn.

In this long street is a most unusual sight. Outside a modern building, transfixed on the tarmac, are three large Victorian gravestones, still bearing the names of those they were intended to mark for ever. These burials took place when the old Free Evangelical Church stood there. In 1968, the old church was demolished and a new one built. The stones were treated with great respect and re-sited along the boundary wall.

'Strike Command' at the north-western end of the village must have swelled the population somewhat, but with fields, meadows and woods easily accessible on either side, the Chiltern scenery is still there in abundance.

Here lived Jack Goodchild, a well-known and skilful chair-maker, who died in 1950. His chairs were much sought after but sadly, Jack did not mark them, and so today there may be many more in existence than is known.

By the middle of the last century, the chair-making indus-try in the nearby town of High Wycombe had grown consid-erably to something like fifty factories, and that number had doubled by the end of the century. The factory owners boasted that they turned out over a million chairs per year. Yet they could not have achieved this figure without the

Bodgers, the men who worked around the Chilterns deep in the beechwoods, turning out the legs for the chairs and keeping the humming factories constantly and rhythmically supplied.

Some worked at this all the year round, some took up thatching and mowing during the summer months and went into the woods when the sap was down and it was possible to fell the timbers. They cleared only a small area of wood at a time and moved about, carefully picking their sites, so that fresh timber was always available to replace the amount they had taken.

Often working alone, or with a boy who was 'larnin'', they erected their primitive shack from the beech boughs and thatched the roof with twigs to keep out the rain, and there, deep in a woodland glade, they axed and sawed, chopped and splintered and turned the chair legs on a pole-lathe worked by a treadle.

The Bodgers were the true men of the woods and the finest exponents of the process of the regeneration of the Chiltern woods.

Nether Winchendon

If ever time has really stood still it is at Nether Winchendon, where the river Thame flows through rich water meadows and cattle stand peacefully along its banks. Where picturesque, half-timbered, thatched cottages cluster, some of them ochre-washed making the scene even more colourful. The interior of the little church of St Nicholas, unlike many other churches, has undergone no restoration or alterations since the early 17th century. The gallery and box pews are still there and date from about 1715. The pulpit with its reading desk and clerk's stall is beautiful, enhanced one summer's day by a simple vase of cow parsley.

The clock in the tower has a pretty blue face and was given by Jane Beresford of Nether Winchendon House (which is open to the public on certain days) and the inscription over the gallery reminds all who hear this clock to 'spend their time in honest discharge of their calling and in the worship of God that repentance may not come too late.'

Standing alone in the church, there came the slow, repetitive sound as of a spade over gravel, which gave the writer some puzzlement, until it was realised that it came from the extreme effort of the 14 ft pendulum as it struggled to follow suit and discharge its duties.

Here in Nether Winchendon in 1540 was born Lettice Knollys, daughter of Sir Francis Knollys and Catherine, niece of Anne Boleyn. Lettice was, therefore, a cousin of Elizabeth I and, as girls, they were very close, but as their lives progressed the age old story of a man came between them.

At the age of 21 Lettice married the first Earl of Essex by whom she had a family and they seemed happy, but he died in 1576, leaving Lettice a beautiful, desirable widow.

At this time Elizabeth was deeply enamoured of Robert Dudley, Earl of Leicester. In fact, it was seriously thought by some that there was a good chance she would marry him, but for one snag – he was already married. Gossip reached fever point when Leicester's wife, Amy, was found dead of a broken neck at the foot of a flight of stairs. Wagging tongues asked was this really an accident and, if not, how much did the Queen know of it? But the astute Elizabeth would never put her crown in danger on a moral issue, or any other for that matter, and she discreetly withdrew and saw less of Leicester, even suggesting that he married Mary, Queen of Scots. Later, to the amazement of everyone, including the Queen, it came to light that he had secretly married Lettice.

Elizabeth's fury knew no bounds, especially with Lettice, and their relationship was never quite the same. Leicester died some ten years later and the beautiful, sought after Lettice could not remain a widow for long. She married Sir Christopher Blount, who was young enough to be her son.

This was not the end of the story for Lettice and the Queen. Their paths crossed yet again when the second Earl of Essex, son of Lettice and her first husband, had grown to manhood. He was particularly handsome, charming and talented, but possessed of a tempestuous and flamboyant nature. Elizabeth, although now ageing, took more than just a passing fancy to him and was said to completely dote upon him. All England knew he was her favourite, but in due course, his sovereign's affection and extreme generosity went to his head.

At the head of some 300 followers, and his stepfather, Sir Christopher Blount, he rode into London shouting slogans in an attempt to overthrow the government. There was no support forthcoming from the people and the mini-revolt was soon over. Essex and Blount were arrested. Lettice went to her cousin, the Queen, and pleaded for their lives, even buying dresses for her with money she could ill afford, to no avail. In 1601 both men were beheaded on Tower Hill. Lettice had lost both husband and son, and her old childhood friend had made no attempt to stop it.

Lettice lived another 33 years, dying at the age of 94. At her death the following epitaph was written:-

> 'There you may see that face, that hand
> Which once was fairest in the land
> She that in her younger years
> Match'd with two great English peers.'

Newport Pagnell

➤ Tickford Bridge at Newport Pagnell, obviously named after the 13th century Tickford Priory, is the oldest cast iron bridge still in daily use by traffic in the country (possibly the world), and was erected about 1810. It spans the river Lovat and the arch is composed of a large number of cast iron segments. It is anchored into stone abutments on each bank, and has received no more than the normal road and bridge maintenance since its erection.

A firm in Rotherham cast the iron and the parts were transported by sea to London, then by the Grand Junction Canal to Great Linford Wharf and from thence conveyed by cart to Newport Pagnell.

It has been said that there are only two of these open

frame voussoir type bridges now in existence – one in Spanish Town, Jamaica and the other here at Newport Pagnell.

Newport Pagnell was an important central garrison for Parliament during the Civil War and Sir Samuel Luke was the Governor here for almost three years. And it was to here, to serve under Luke, that a young sixteen year old lad came. His name was John Bunyan.

Also here was stationed Oliver, son of Oliver Cromwell, who held the rank of Captain. He was the 'apple of his father's eye' being 'a civil young gentleman'. Unfortunately, at Newport Pagnell, he fell victim to the smallpox and died in 1644, to the everlasting distress of his father.

Newton Blossomville

➤ 'The Old Mill that Burned Down' must surely be the only pub in the country, let alone the county, where 'Time' is called from a pulpit! And what an intriguing name!

Apparently, a mill once stood on this site which was converted into a pub and aptly called 'The Old Mill'. Then, in the early 1980s, a mysterious fire completely destroyed the building and, after it had been rebuilt into the attractive place it is now, someone hit on the very bright idea of being clinically descriptive and called it 'The Old Mill That Burned Down'.

The customer, whilst quietly sipping and contemplating, suddenly becomes aware that there is something markedly different about the bar. It is of oak, richly and beautifully carved with Tudor roses etc, and it comes as no surprise to be informed that it was once the pulpit in a Midland cathedral.

This village certainly lives up to its pretty name with attractive stone cottages plus the warm friendliness of the inhabitants. It acquired the name from the Blossomville family who held land here in 1203, and it is the last village on the river Ouse before it flows out of the county into Bedfordshire. The little school, built by a curate, is opposite the church, close by a patch of green, and the playground adjoins the churchyard.

The lofty church of St Nicholas consists of a mixture of styles but is mostly 13th century. It is made even more attractive by the presence of the Ouse which skirts the churchyard to the rear. A path runs down to an idyllic spot where the river breaks up into many streams that pass under quite a junction of curved bridges going this way and that. Here reeds cluster and kingcups bloom, trout of all sizes frolic teased perpetually by flashing dragonflies and brilliant kingfishers. The gentle river moves slowly on, trees of all shades bowing along its banks as it glides out of the county, creating one of the most beautiful spots imaginable.

It is interesting to note that William Warburton was rector here for just two years, 1726 to 1728. He was always writing and forever up to his neck in some kind of controversy. He was the literary executor of Alexander Pope and brought out his own edition of Shakespeare's works which was more than heavily criticised. He was described by his contemporaries as 'a bad scholar, arrogant, a bully, and a man of untrustworthy character.' He ended up as Bishop of Gloucester.

North Marston

Rector John Schorne moved from the living of Monks Risborough church to that of North Marston in 1290 and remained there until his death in 1314. During that time, he made more of an impact than most rectors, to say the least. Referred to and addressed as either Sir or Master John Schorne, he became known far and wide for his miraculous powers and his piety was so extreme that it was written 'his knees became horny, from the frequency of his prayers.' After his death, he was looked upon as a saint, though unofficial, and people came to his shrine at North Marston for over two centuries afterwards.

To achieve this status and fame he performed two great miracles. He is said to have struck the ground with his staff, whereupon a spring blessed with amazing healing powers gushed forth. Helped along by his prayers and benedictions,

John Schorne's Well, North Marston

the water was said to cure gout, ague, rheumatism and afflictions of the eye. Sufferers from these ailments and others came from far and wide to the well which stood and still stands some 150 yards from the church down 'Schorne Lane'. A box was prudently attached to a nearby wall where grateful sufferers could place a donation and the small village of North Marston flourished on the proceeds.

By 1835, the water from the well had become the water supply for the entire village and, shortly after, when a cholera epidemic hit the county, the people of North Marston remained remarkably free of infection, which was attributed to the medicinal qualities of the water. Doctors in nearby towns and villages were known to prescribe the well water to patients. It was thought at one stage, however, that the medicinal qualities may have been weakened somewhat when one old lady fell into the well and drowned. Thereafter it was covered over.

The second miracle by John Schorne brought him even more fame than the last. He performed the hair-raising feat of conjuring and imprisoning the Devil in a boot, hence the rhyme:

'Master Schorne,
That blessed man born,
Who conjured the Devil into a Boot.'

Pictures of the great man holding his boot containing the Devil were depicted on screens, painted windows and in sculpture in various parts of England, not to mention the inn sign of the Devil in the Boot public house at nearby Winslow.

John Schorne was buried in North Marston church and pilgrims came in droves to visit his shrine, cottages in the village providing accommodation. Some came as an act of devotion and some were ordered to do so as penance, but whatever the reason the Dean of Windsor did not think much of it and, in an effort to capture some of the lucrative trade, he had the shrine removed to Windsor. It did not work and eventually John Schorne was returned to his resting place.

In 1947 some bones were found in a small recess in the church which were thought to be connected with the relics of John Schorne.

Browne Willis, a county historian working in the 18th century, reported a meeting he had with John Virgin, a later vicar of North Marston, who described to him a picture of John Schorne that was once displayed inside the church. The miracle-worker was painted with a boot under his arm, like a bag-pipe, into which he was squeezing a moppet, representing the Devil. There had also been a statue of Schorne and it was considered likely that attached to it was a mechanical device which enabled the 'Devil' to pop in and out of the boot to the wonderment of spectators. This may have been the origin of the popular toy, the 'Jack in the Box'.

The John Virgin referred to is the subject of a remarkable and amusing tablet in the chancel. Recounting the details of his life and his death in 1694, a hand and finger point downwards to the floor and an inscription informs us that 'He Lise gust downe thare.'

The chancel was restored by Queen Victoria after the death of the Buckinghamshire miser, John Camden Neild, who left her his entire fortune of over half a million pounds, although he had never so much as set eyes on her.

A further interesting item to be seen on a shelf at the back of the church is the mechanism of the old church tower clock, dated about 1730, weight driven and probably made locally, and surprisingly in use until 1985.

Olney

In the mid 1800s the cottage industry of lace making was to be found all over the county and its makers were very proud of the Buckinghamshire Lace, which they were, and are, convinced is the most beautiful of all lace. Women started young in a Lace School, where the teacher taught the youngest and supervised the older girls. In winter, they placed pots of hot coals under their stools, their voluminous skirts forming a tent all round to keep their legs and feet warm. Lace dealers collected the lace from some villages and took it into the centres to sell.

To pin down exactly when or how pillow lace making was first introduced into the county is very difficult. Certainly tradition has it that Queen Catherine of Aragon did so in the 16th century and there is a Spanish-style lace known as Catherine of Aragon lace. There is also a stitch called 'Kat stitch' which is said to have been created by her.

However it may have been that Flemish immigrants arriving here having fled from persecution during the Spanish occupation of the Low Countries brought their lace making skills with them. It seems that a combination of both sources lent flavour and style. In the last two centuries, there was hardly a village in the whole of Buckinghamshire where women did not sit outside their cottage doors with bobbins dangling on a huge pillow making the lace.

Machine-made lace came along in the second half of the

19th century and brought about something of a decline in the cottage industry, but then it perked up again. In 1901 in the village of Hanslope it is recorded that 800 people out of a population of 1,275 were engaged in lace making and at that time they were turning it out at Stoke Goldington near Olney as well. So much so that a man named H. H. Armstrong started the Bucks Cottage Workers Association in the hopes of re-organising the industry. His lace makers were given materials and buyers came from all over to acquire the completed work. The standard of workmanship was not only maintained but even improved to such an extent that by 1909 it was decided to move the scheme from Stoke Goldington to Olney, the larger town with better rail and postal services. The circularised catalogue of work was extensive. Complete christening and wedding gowns were produced together with work for Queen Alexandra and the Princess Royal. At the Festival of Empire and Exhibition held at the Crystal Palace, the lace from Olney was given a Gold Medal.

It is in Olney High Street that there is a very tangible reminder of that later peak of lace making in the early part of this century, the revival brought about by H. H. Armstrong. It is a building specially erected at that time as a lace factory, on the front of which, high above the door and on the second floor, are the words 'Bucks Lace Industry' and above that, in an arch, is depicted the traditional old Bucks lace maker sitting with her equipment, her pillow and her bobbins. There is also a section of the Cowper and Newton Museum dedicated to the pillow lace for which Olney was once an important centre.

The craft is not dead for the lace makers of Buckinghamshire. They can still be found keeping the old patterns going, even if today it is more of a hobby.

Prestwood

➤ Down the little lane that leads from Prestwood to Hampden, just opposite Honour End Farm and overlooking the beautiful Hampden valley, is a stone memorial in the

Memorial to John Hampden, Prestwood

shape of a Maltese Cross. It was set up in 1863 by Lord Chief
Justice Erle to the memory of Buckinghamshire's greatest
hero, John Hampden (1594–1643), and to his refusal in 1635
to pay the Ship Money 'levied by command of the King
without Authority of the Law'. This was one of the most
significant and courageous acts in the history of England and
formed part of the chain of events that led to the Civil War.

John Hampden was much loved by his friends and neighbours throughout the county even before this event. He was a good, straight, honest man 'in whose loyalty we ever had good cause to confide.' He came from an ancient Buckinghamshire family and had not his grandfather, old Griffith Hampden, entertained Queen Elizabeth I at Hampden House? Cousin to Oliver Cromwell and Edmund Waller, John had been educated at Thame and Oxford. As Justice of the Peace and MP for Wendover through five Parliaments, he had performed his duty as he thought fit, without fear or favour from any man. His conduct and brilliance in the House brought the admiration and respect of all men when he represented the County.

The memorial stands on lands that were owned by him and, until 1852, formed part of Stoke Mandeville. It was on these lands that he was assessed and refused to pay the sum of 20 shillings. It was a paltry amount to the wealthy Hampden, but he chose to stand by his belief in Parliamentary control of taxes and the freedom of the individual. It led to a state trial which argued the validity of Ship Money.

From then on all lovers of freedom looked to him and, when the Civil War began, he gathered men of Buckinghamshire around him and formed a regiment of Bucks militia – the famous 'Green Coats'. He received wounds at the Battle of Chalgrove Field in 1643 which led to his death a week later at nearby Thame. He was buried in Great Hampden church, right next to Hampden House.

Over the centuries it has been seriously wondered by some learned historians whether, had Hampden lived, the life of the King would have been forfeited as it was that day in Whitehall in 1649. His cousin Cromwell could well have done with his restraining influence at the end of the war.

Look hard for this monument, or you will miss it, and step into its fenced enclosure through the little gate, not forgetting to admire the view of the countryside this great man of Buckinghamshire knew and loved so well.

Soulbury

➤ The Lovett family of nearby Liscombe Park ruled the roost here for many centuries. One member of the family was Master of Wolf Hounds to William the Conqueror, which is why that animal is part of the family crest. The church, standing high on a hillock above the pretty village, is not short of Lovett memorials, all of interest and high quality, but the one the visitor may be pleasurably surprised to see is that to Robert Lovett, Sheriff of Buckinghamshire, who died in 1690. It was put up by his daughter, Lettice, in 1701 and is the work of none other than Grinling Gibbons (1648–1720), who is generally acknowledged as the greatest wood-carver of all time. He also worked in marble and attained high distinction as a sculptor. He became Master Carver in Wood to the Crown, a post he held from the reign of Charles II to that of George I. His work appears in the most awesome of places such as St Paul's Cathedral, Windsor and Whitehall. Needless to say, his carvings were much sought after and nearly all the mansions of the aristocracy built at this time were decorated by or under Gibbons.

Here at Soulbury they have been doubly lucky for in All Saints church they have the best of both Gibbons' worlds. The memorial, depicting an urn and cherubs, is in marble, but high on the top is a woodcarving – the black wolf of the Lovetts.

Hardly hidden, bang in the middle of the road, in front of the splendid Lovetts' School of 1724 and near the church, is a huge stone, which some may say is a traffic hazard. It is in fact a glacial erratic left behind by the last ice-sheet when it withdrew to the north at the end of the glacial epoch. It is difficult to imagine this landscape looking like Antarctica some 13,000 years ago, but as this ice-sheet rolled south, it is said to have been stopped short by the main escarpment of the Chiltern Hills. Then, as the climate slowly warmed up, the ice began to recede leaving behind rocks and debris that it had carried with it, sometimes for hundreds of miles. The one at Soulbury is a good example of Derbyshire Millstone

Grit, a coarse sandstone used for making millstones in the past.

However, local tradition has it that the stone rolled to Soulbury by itself and that at certain times it rolls down the hill and – wait for it – rolls up again. Whether this movement has actually been witnessed by any sober informant is not known.

It may be that the people of Soulbury attained a rock-like determination from this stone in the middle of their village. In the 1960s, it was decided to site a third London Airport here, with this lovely countryside, including the villages of Stewkley, Wing and others, forming the centre. The people of the area made a determined stand, formed many opposing organisations and, joined by the Buckinghamshire County Council, put up a fight the like of which had never been seen before. The picturesque villages were covered with posters, banners and slogans – 'Save our Soulbury' was a very apt one – and there were massive demonstrations. One never to be forgotten was when hundreds of farmers, driving their tractors, converged on Stewkley. It is not often that victory goes to the people, but this time they won. The celebrations were tremendous, and a gigantic torchlight procession made its way to Stewkley church to give thanks.

Steeple Claydon

Here is the barn around which Cromwell's soldiers camped the night before the attack on Hillesden House at the beginning of March, 1644. It is in the main street nearly opposite the road to Buckingham and is adorned with a large plaque dated 8th August 1857 which reads:

The Camp Barn
Around this spot the Army of Parliament, under the command of Cromwell, was encamped March 1644 and on the 3rd of that month advanced from hence to the attack on Hillesden House.

Barn at Steeple Claydon

The mellow old stone barn is small and can have changed but little since that night the soldiers spent here nearly 350 years ago, perhaps singing hymns and feeling nervous about the proposed encounter on the morrow. Although it is approximately five miles by road from here to Hillesden, it is only a matter of one mile across the fields, which is undoubtedly the route they would have taken using Hillesden church tower as a guide.

Steeple Claydon is the largest of the Claydon villages and stands on a hill. The Chaloner family held the manor in Stuart times and Sir Thomas Chaloner was tutor to Prince Henry, son of James I. The next Sir Thomas, a staunch Parliamentarian, was one of the King's judges and went so far as to sign the death warrant of Charles I. Therefore, it was not entirely unexpected when at the Restoration of the Monarchy he was required to forfeit his estate to a gentleman who had helped Charles II to escape after the battle of

138

Worcester. But the indefatigable Chaloners bought the manor back only a few years later.

Thomas Chaloner founded the school here in 1656. As late as 1827 the ghastly practice of bull baiting was taking place in the schoolyard, hence the name Bull Lane.

In the 19th century, the Verney family extended the school, forming the village hall and library. The Claydon villages were the first to adopt the Public Libraries Act and Florence Nightingale gave a cheque for £50 as a contribution towards this. That cheque bearing this great lady's signature hangs in a frame on the wall to this day.

Swan Bottom

In this part of the Chilterns, largely made up of wooded ridges and waterless bottoms, it is easy to become lost in the network of small lanes that twist and turn, rise and dip, and link the many small villages around. Yet that was not exactly what happened to *Duchess* that day in mid July 1907.

Drayman Jim Gilbert had delivered beer to the Red Lion inn at Lee Common and, in the early afternoon, set off along the winding, leafy lanes towards Swan Bottom. *Duchess*, the lead horse of the two that pulled his dray, was a smart animal. She knew her way around this maze of ways and what's more, she knew all the pubs in the area to which Wellers Brewery delivered. The other horse followed her implicitly and *Duchess* could be completely relied upon to keep her in order and the dray on the left side of the road.

It was a warm, sunny day and, without a doubt, Jim had enjoyed his free pint of beer at the Red Lion. He had been up since four in the morning, doing his chores in his little cottage back in Amersham, looking after his seven children who had lost their mother just a few years before. He had started on his round at half past five and he was tired. The reins were hitched up to an arrangement like a metal horn at his side and, just for safety, Jim placed his leg over them and leaned back on to a barrel at the back of him, two more on either side providing a well with arms. The jiggety-jog of the horses' ambling gait ran a lulling rhythm in his head. 'Good Old *Duchess*', he thought.

On through the lanes they went, down the dip into Swan Bottom and on between high hedges until at last they came to a small crossroads. *Duchess* must have hesitated. Should she turn up right to the Old Swan, or was she expected to go straight on to the Gate Inn just above Wendover? She went straight on.

Glancing out of the window of the Gate Inn, the landlady was surprised to see *Duchess* pull the dray off the road into the small lane leading to the pub, as if delivering. The dray hit a post which woke Jim with a start. Where was he? The landlady called out that she had not ordered any beer and Jim sleepily replied that his load was not for her but for the Old Swan, and that he must have been asleep all along Swan Bottom. He called on a gawping lad standing by to turn *Duchess* back on to the road. The boy grabbed her head and the next moment, Jim, his feet and legs encased in reins, was pulled from the dray, his head in the direct path of the left front wheel. It happened in the twinkling of an eye, the wheel going over his head.

They sent for a doctor from Wendover and Jim lived for just another three hours. Back at those crossroads, his beloved *Duchess* had made an error of judgement that had been fatal to her master and also changed the course of the lives of seven children. Yet who could blame her? Certainly Jim would not have done so.

The Old Swan is still there and so is the Gate Inn, but the Red Lion became a private house many years ago. And the story of Jim and his *Duchess* would more than likely have been well and truly forgotten but for one fact – he was the writer's grandfather.

Tattenhoe

➤ The most difficult of places to find and certainly the most remote. It has been said that Tattenhoe is one of the smallest villages in the whole of the country, if indeed village it may be called.

Through the gate of Home Park Farm, a single track stretches for something like a mile until just two or three houses stand in a little knot. A right turn through another gate, possibly tied up with string, and passing ponds on either side of the way, the track continues until brought abruptly to a halt by open fields. Here, hidden behind a copse of trees and surrounded by countryside, may be found the tiny church of St Giles.

It very nearly fills the churchyard, brick buttresses support the sagging walls and a little wooden bellcote adorns the roof. Peering through the windows, the interior seems plain and simple with box pews and nave and chancel rolled into one. Amid the yew trees, there are two or three gravestones dating back to the 1920s and nut trees overhang the church-yard walls.

The church has no electricity or heating. Therefore, it is not surprising that church services begin only at Pentecost and are held every other Sunday through to Harvest. One Communion service is held per year. During the winter months the church is virtually inaccessible through swollen ponds and thick clay fields.

There was once a chapel here that belonged to nearby Snelshall Priory and the founder of that priory, Ralph Mar-tel, was granted the manor of Tattenhoe by King John in 1255. In the 16th century Henry VIII gave orders that the priory was to be demolished. The chapel fell into disuse and became derelict. The present church was built in 1540 with stones from the ruins of the priory. It stands very near the site of the old manor house and parts of the moat and ancient fishponds are still to be seen in close proximity.

The population of the parish of Tattenhoe, standing on the east side of Whaddon Chase, did not exceed 22 persons during a period of some 300 years. In the reorganisation of local government in 1974, it ceased to be and merged with the parish of Shenley Brook End.

It can safely be promised that a visitor will not forget Tattenhoe church, standing alone and forlorn amid miles of unbroken countryside nursing its secrets of the past.

Medieval Bridge at Thornborough

Thornborough

➤ |Standing on this, the sole surviving medieval bridge in Buckinghamshire, one can almost hear the sound of the wheels that have trundled across, from the primitive carts of early times to the stage coaches of the 19th century, and even modern day traffic, although the narrowness of the bridge compelled a single line flow and often slowed down irate

drivers to a snail's pace. For it was only in recent years that a new bridge was built a short distance upstream allowing the busy A421 to bypass the old one so as to ensure its preservation for posterity.

It was built of local stone in the 14th century and has been restored from time to time. It is 165 ft long and 12 ft wide and has six arches, three of which are ribbed. Through them runs the Claydon Brook, a tributary of the river Ouse. This bridge also supports the old boundary stone of Thornborough with Buckingham and has small embrasures where people can stand to gaze down into the reeds and softly flowing waters.

From this spot you will be staggered to see two huge grass covered mounds, some 25 ft high. Upon being opened up by the Duke of Buckingham in around 1840 they were found to contain the richest series of Romano-British remains explored up until that date. So opulently furnished were these barrows that they suggested the presence at that time of a local native aristocracy and the great importance of this crossing and consequently of Thornborough.

The finds unearthed are now in the University Museum of Archaeology and Ethnology at Cambridge and included a small bronze lamp with its wick still in place, a large jug of greenish glass, Roman coins, a terra sigillata bowl, the hilt of a sword, a large glass vessel or urn which contained ashes and fragments of bones and various other jugs, lamps and dishes. Last but not least was found an ornament of purest gold with the figure of Cupid skilfully and elegantly chased upon it.

Nearby traces were found of a temple, thought to have been erected around AD 256, together with several cremation burials.

Turville

➤ There was no fairytale, handsome Prince to awaken the 'sleeping girl' of Turville with a kiss. And so she slept on until it seemed that nothing and no-one could ever rouse her from her nine and a half year sleep.

Ellen Sadler was born in 1859 and was the tenth child of a family of twelve that lived in one of the cottages in close proximity to the pretty church and churchyard. Up until she was eleven years old, she had been perfectly healthy and normal in every way. She was not a dullard at school and enjoyed church and Sunday school to the full. She was quiet and thoughtful and, in all, of so sweet a nature as to be dubbed by some of her friends a 'goody-goody'. There was absolutely no sign or indication of what was to come.

As was the custom, at an early age she was sent off into service as a nursemaid at Marlow and it was whilst she was there that she first developed symptoms of drowsiness to such a degree that it seemed unnatural and uncontrollable. She complained of a pain in her head and a local doctor advised her parents to send her to Reading Hospital. Here she remained for the term of 17 weeks, after which she was sent back to Turville on a bed in a cart and proclaimed incurable.

Even under her mother's care, her condition deteriorated and the bouts of somnolence grew more frequent and of longer duration. She seldom spoke nor seemed to have the slightest interest in anything around her, though now and again she went off into a fit of hysterics.

On 29th March 1871, she remarked that she could hear bells in her head and then went into a series of convulsions. By the time the doctor had arrived, she had lapsed into a sleep that was to last over nine years.

During this time, she never once moved her position herself and, although her jaw became clenched, she was fed by her mother with regular doses of port wine and sugar through a gap in her teeth with the aid of a small teapot three times a day. The liquid passed straight down the throat without any sign of swallowing. Her breathing was regular, her body warm and she had a pleasant look on her face.

As time wore on, people came from far and wide to view what was considered to be one of the most inexplicable, physiological phenomena known. Among them were eminent physicians who, although full of complex medical terms, came up with no definite conclusions. The local doctor was of the opinion that the girl was paralysed and quite unconscious, whereas the vicar felt that 'the mental was not quite so torpid as the bodily power'. All those that came to see 'the sleeping girl' rarely left without leaving some financial recompense for Mother.

The neighbours and local people looked askance and were sceptical. They thought it was a clever swindle and that Mother was on to a lucrative game. Nevertheless, it would be difficult to credit that a young girl would lie in such a position for nine years without moving or speaking. And, anyway, it must have cost Mother a pretty penny in port wine!

In the May of 1880, the mother died suddenly and an

Inquest was held at the Bull and Butcher in the village which caused yet another stir. Although it was the death of the mother that was under examination, it being resolved that she died from natural causes, the main concern of the kindly Coroner appears to have been for the welfare of Ellen who was left still sleeping on her bed with no-one to attend her. Her step-father needed to go to work, but her sister who lived next door stated that she would attend her.

Whether it was the fact that the sister stepped up the doses of port wine and milk, sometimes varied with tea, to every hour on the hour, is not certain, but the condition of Ellen began to improve and by the following December, she was able to sit up and talk. She could remember nothing of the time she had been slumbering and spoke and acted like the child that had first gone to sleep, although she was now 21.

Improvement continued and she was examined by medical men who swore there was nothing strange about her appearance or condition, save for the fact that at first she could only open one eye. She continued to live in the village with her married sister and took up bead work for a living.

Allison Uttley states that years later she met an old man, with a knowing chuckle, who told her that 'the sleeping girl of Turville' eventually married and had twins.

Tylers Green

➤ A newcomer to this pleasant green may become quite bemused to find it encircled not by one village but two. At one end is the village of Penn and the frequently visited Cottage Bookshop, and at the other that of Tylers Green with seemingly no gap between. Yet the boundary runs straight through the pond on the green and is also the Saxon boundary dividing the Chiltern Hundreds of Desborough and Burnham. At one time, from these two villages so closely entwined came almost all the tiles used in South Buckinghamshire – hence the name Tylers Green. They provided flooring for many local churches, the Palace of Westminster and even Windsor Castle.

The pond is large, well-kept and home to many ducks of varying shades and sizes that rush and squawk for food when a visitor draws near. On the green is a seat made from the trunk of a fir tree of considerable girth that stood for many years in the grounds of the little school opposite. It grew so large that someone became alarmed that it might fall on the building itself.

There once was a house called Tylers Green House where in 1796 Edmund Burke (1729–97) the great politician and author of *Reflections on the French Revolution*, founded a school for approximately 60 French children who had lost their father or near relations to the guillotine. They wore a uniform of blue and in their hats a white cockade inscribed 'Vive le Roi'. Burke, who lived at nearby Beaconsfield, frequently visited the school, sending produce from his farm to help sustain the growing appetites. When, in later years, he began to feel a decline in health, he worried over what would happen to the school and his little charges after his death. He approached his friend Pitt and a Government grant of £600 per annum was made to the school until all the troubles in France were well and truly over and it was safe to send the pupils back to their homeland. The house was then sold by auction and demolished.

But the educational tradition carries on at the large house of Rayners, now a school for the deaf. It was built by Sir Philip Rose as his dream house in 1847. He had been born in the town of Wycombe in 1816 into a family well-known in this part of the county; his brother, father, grandfather and great-grandfather all having been mayors of that town in their time. In early boyhood he formed a friendship with the young Benjamin Disraeli who lived at nearby Bradenham Manor and the attachment remained lifelong. He helped Disraeli in the elections and became so practised in the art that he was made National Agent for the Conservative Party. He was a clever solicitor and his work included much that was parliamentary, such as drafting reform bills etc, and he personally handled all Disraeli's legal and financial affairs.

He purchased Rayners Farm and other land in 1845 and commenced to build the house. It turned out to be a well-designed residence, set in beautiful gardens with parkland, woods and plantations. The house has now been extended for the new school and the buildings are grouped around a courtyard. Disraeli admired it and on his last journey to Hughenden called at Rayners to see his old friend. Later, Sir Philip was one of those present at his death.

Queen Victoria later wished to follow the same route through Rayners to Hughenden that her favourite Minister had taken on his last journey home. She was met in her carriage by a groom at the gate and conducted through the grounds to the front door and so on to the gate leading to Hughenden where she laid a wreath of primroses on the tomb.

Sir Philip also built the little church of St Margaret at Tylers Green in 1854. However, the turret was added after his death in 1891 and is notable for its tall bell stage which is entirely of wood with tracery.

Waddesdon

➤ Visitors throng to enjoy the treasures and atmosphere of Waddesdon Manor, built by Baron Ferdinand de Roth-schild towards the end of the 19th century, and rightly so. And, though in such close proximity, the Church of St Michael in the village is so often overlooked. Entered through the Norman doorway, the overall effect of the interior is extremely beautiful. The outstanding pulpit of alabaster came from Blenheim Palace and was presented to the church by the Duke of Marlborough. It is said to have been purchased at the Great Exhibition of 1851.

Behind the pulpit, and perhaps the most impressive possession of all, once the story is known, is the brass of Sir Roger Dynham of Eythrope, at nearby Upper Winchenden, who died in 1490. The brass is quite large and measures six feet by three. It was probably made to the orders of Sir Roger himself long before his actual death, as it was quite common practice at that time to design your own memorial so as to ensure it was just what you wanted when your time came.

Sir Roger stipulated in his will that his body was to be

buried in Waddesdon Church until his chantry chapel at Eythrope was completed. After that, he required his remains to be transported from Waddesdon to that chapel and there to lie together with his brass in peace for all time. These instructions were adhered to and, despite the fact that by 1550 Henry VIII had destroyed every chantry in England, Roger's little building at Eythrope was allowed to remain as a private chapel attached to the house.

All seemed well, and the Eythrope estate passed first into the hands of the Dormer family and then on to the Stanhopes. However, in 1738 Sir William Stanhope, second son of the third Earl of Chesterfield, upset the Bucks antiquarian, Browne Willis, by 'most wickedly, sacrilegiously, and impiously' demolishing the chapel and added insult to injury by making use of the stones from it to build a bridge over the river Thame near his mansion. Not only that, he went so far as to use them as a rockery at Beachendon manor farm. Worst of all, poor Sir Roger's coffin was broken open by looters.

Time passed, and the sixth Earl of Chesterfield nursed ambitions to become Lord Lieutenant of the County. There was no reason to suppose that he would not. In 1810 he threw a party at Eythrope and was more than a little set back when one of the guests greeted him with the news that Lord Cobham had been promised the sought-after office. Lord Chesterfield went immediately into a fit of pique, broke up the party, left the County and never set foot in it again. Soon afterwards he gave instructions that the house was to be demolished, and so it was!

The estate was purchased in 1875 by Miss Alice de Rothschild who built a pavilion of a house close to the site of the old building.

But what, you may ask, of Sir Roger after all these years? Miss Alice was more than a little worried when it came to her ears that a night watchman at Eythrope had imparted the news that a particular part of the grounds was haunted and, even in those days when employment was precious, flatly refused to go anywhere near a certain spot where no grass would grow.

Miss Alice, in an effort to placate the ruffled feelings of the night watchman, arranged for the topsoil to be removed. Less than a foot below the surface was found a coffin of lead containing the skeleton of a man. With it was the enormous brass that now resides in Waddesdon church, and the body was identified as that of Sir Roger.

Miss Alice had the bones of Sir Roger re-interred in Waddesdon churchyard and the brass was set in its present place in the church. After a period of some 400 years, Sir Roger had returned to his original resting place.

Whaddon

The church of St Mary at Whaddon has six bells and a sanctus, and all save one were cast by either Anthony, George or Richard Chandler in the 17th and early 18th century at their bell foundry at nearby Drayton Parslow. Therefore, it is not surprising that the fascinating weight-driven clock mechanism that stands on an oak horse just inside the north door was made by Anthony Chandler. The whole is some five feet high and at first sight looks like the work of a mad inventor. But it is far from that. It was worked by weights on the end of ropes wound round the oak drums, and more often than not, clocks of this type were made by blacksmiths. Anthony's father, Richard, began his working life as a smith.

A plate in the nearby window states that the clock was given to the church by Amy Emerton, the married daughter of the Reverend John Allen, vicar of Whaddon from 1587 to 1643, and adds 'Anthony Chandler made me 1673'. It is an absolute gem to find in the corner of a village church.

And this is not the only unusual item in the church. The 13th century font is tub shaped on four ornamented shafts. The lid is now of wood, carved by Pugh of Wolverhampton, and was dedicated as late as 1956. But look up and above at the pulley which was used for raising the lid in the days when it was of stone. The end of the bracket that holds the pulley is a carved dog's head, said to be the work of a village

The 13th century Font at Whaddon Church

craftsman who used as a model the head of 'mine own cur' of whom he was obviously very fond.

The village of Whaddon stands on a high plateau some 500 ft above sea level and from the churchyard there are extensive views of the undulating hunting country of Whaddon Chase.

A Chase was usually a detached portion of a royal forest granted to a subject by a Sovereign and to which the usual forest laws did not apply. Whaddon Chase was granted by Henry III and was supposed to be large enough to feed a thousand head of deer. Today all that is left of the old forest are a few pieces of woodland.

The village seems full of modern houses, but this may be because the manor was scattered and only in comparatively recent years have houses sprung up near the church and Hall. Browne Willis, the antiquary and historian of Buckinghamshire, lived and died here at Whaddon Hall in the 18th century and he always swore that it was under an old oak tree in the grounds that Spenser wrote his *Faerie Queene* around 1580. Willis based this largely on the fact that the writer had been secretary to Lord Grey de Wilton, the owner of the Hall at the time.

Whitchurch

Walter Bolebec was one of the assessors of the Domesday survey, which was no mean feat even by today's standards. And the Conqueror was so pleased with his meticulous efforts that he gave him the manor of Whitchurch which lies on the main Aylesbury-Buckingham road on a ridge of hills that affords splendid views of the Vale of Aylesbury.

The manor was held under him by a relative, Hugh de Bolebec, who is said by some to be the man who built Bolebec Castle, although there is some confusion as to whether the founder of the Castle was this Hugh or his son of the same name.

Not many of those who travel through Whitchurch today are aware that the ancient earthworks of this once important castle lie close to the main road, out of sight behind the quaint cottages that form the west side of the High Street. They may be reached by turning off and down Market Hill, taking a left turn into Castle Lane which runs between the mounds of the Castle. There are plenty of public footpaths traversing the earthworks from which they may be viewed at the same time providing an extremely pleasant walk with views of Whitchurch and the Vale.

The remains of the castle give a good idea of the shape of what was once a univallate hill-fort occupying a 16 acre site. The mound is steep and imposing. In the mind's eye, one can almost see the high outer wall with turrets rising from the green hillocks, and a bailey surrounded by a moat. The barbican tower housed the drawbridge and gave access to the inner keep.

Came the Civil War in the 17th century and the castle had fallen into a state of disrepair. Nevertheless, it still stood proudly for the Royalist cause, until the Roundheads gave it a good pounding and virtually laid it waste. In came the local builders who made the most of the rubble lying around, carting it off and using the stones from the once mighty Bolebec Castle to build the walls of houses and barns, not to mention the repair of many a local church, including Wing. However, it is said that the foundations and drawbridge could still be seen up until 1815.

When these earthworks were excavated human skeletons were found, also quite a few cannonballs and a large stone fireplace still holding the embers of a fire.

A spring by the lovely name of 'Fair Alice' once served the moat and still may be seen on the eastern side, flowing and trickling over the stones from the roots of a large ash tree, creating a scene as of a fairy grotto. It is said to be named after Alice de Bolebec who found the waters beneficial to her health.

The village of Whitchurch is most attractive with tiny lanes off the main road filled with a variety of picturesque cottages built in many different materials. The way to the church, which dominates the village, is particularly pleasing, passing the 15th century timber-framed Priory with oversailing upper floor.

Whiteleaf

➤ The Cross itself, cut into the chalk turf on a spur of the Chiltern Hills, is certainly not hidden. In fact, from its position on a steep slope above the hamlet of Whiteleaf on the Upper Icknield Way, it can be seen for some 30 miles and from various parts of the Vale of Aylesbury. It has even been claimed that it can be glimpsed from Magdalen Tower, Oxford.

From the car park on the summit of the hill, the Ridgeway path leads to the top of the Cross, which is said to be 80 ft across and stands on a triangular base. From the fields above, owned by the National Trust, there may be obtained the most spectacular views of the Buckinghamshire countryside.

The origins of the Cross, however, are well and truly hidden in the mists of time and speculation.

There are those who say that the site was occupied by some kind of boundary mark as long ago as AD 903 but that the actual cross is of a much later date and may well be the work of medieval monks residing at Monks Risborough or Missenden Abbey. Then there is the fact that above the Cross is a Neolithic barrow which, upon excavation between 1935 and 1939, was found to contain the body of a man, aged around 35, in a wooden burial chamber. One theory holds that the Cross may have originally been a phallic symbol and the arms added later.

Of course, the Danes come into it – when don't they? Some say the Cross was cut to commemorate a victory of the Saxons over the Danes, and then again others say it was the other way round. It was a victory of the Danes over the Saxons. Another group aver it was purely an Anglo-Saxon mark for the benefit of travellers.

Not content with speculating in those early times, yet another school of thought says it is no older than the 17th century and cut by Cavaliers of the Royal garrison at Oxford to serve as a landmark in their Chiltern operations during the Civil War. But no, say others, it was not the work of

Royalists but of their adversaries, the Parliamentary troops, in order to indicate to those stationed in the Vale 'the route, by way of Hampden and Missenden, to the Headquarters of the Bucks Lieutenants at Amersham. Probably it formed part of Hampden's general scheme of defence for the Chiltern Hills, which protected London from the King's threatened advance.'

Whatever and whichever, the Cross was preserved by an Inclosure Act at the time of George IV. It was incorporated in the arms of the County in 1947 and is now to be found on the official list of ancient monuments.

No matter how many antiquarians and archaeologists hold their fevered brows in puzzlement over this elusive relic, it has been a source of fun and festivity for the local people over the years. For the Cross has to be scoured from time to time – its outline kept clean. In the past, the villagers of Monks Risborough and surrounds have put aside a day and made this job an excuse for great merrymaking, and at one time the Oxford Colleges joined them.

Woodrow

When the long-awaited bypass came to the old town of Amersham, it completely severed Cherry Lane, a turning off the High Street and the pretty way to Woodrow, a tiny hamlet some two miles away. It can now only be reached from the opposite side, the A404 road to High Wycombe.

The old name for Woodrow was 'wuda raw', meaning 'the way through the wood'. And so it was, for the length of Cherry Lane was one of the loveliest walks in the neighbourhood with extensive woods on either side, giving way to unfolding views of the surrounding hills.

Once a manor in its own right, until taken over by the neighbouring manor of Shardeloes around the end of the 17th century, Woodrow consisted of a collection of farms and brick and timbered cottages, most of which have now been made into attractive homes.

There was once a small school serving the hamlet and also

a Particular Baptist chapel. The records show that those attending this chapel at Woodrow were considered a disorderly lot by others of the same denomination in the district and whether this was the reason that the Rev Richard Morris was appointed their pastor in 1776 is not known. He seemed pleased at the time, but the moment the new chapel in the town of Amersham was built in 1779, he moved there.

Woodrow High House, presumably once the manor house, is largely 17th century and undoubtedly the hamlet's crown. It is set in well wooded grounds noted for rare specimen trees. Here it is that Mrs Oliver Cromwell and her daughters lived for a while.

The house has had a succession of owners over the centuries. In 1946 it was presented to the London Federation of Boys Clubs as a training centre to enable youngsters from the inner cities not only to get to know and enjoy the countryside, but to take part in courses in self-development and social and leadership skills. Today the house and woods resound to their young voices. But that is not all – there is also the sound of the rustling skirts and sobs of The Green Lady, Lady Helena Stanhope, a ward of one of the past owners of the house. And thereby hangs the tale of one of the best ghost stories in the district, and it goes back to the time of the Duke of Monmouth's rebellion against the reign of his uncle, James II.

Monmouth had landed at Lyme in Dorset in June 1685 and gathered his followers around him as champion of the Protestant cause. However, it was not long before his forces were totally routed at Sedgemoor, where he was caught and executed. Most of his followers who were not killed in the battle suffered at the Bloody Assizes conducted by the monstrous Judge Jeffreys. But one of Monmouth's followers, Sir Peter Bostock, escaped and, eluding his pursuers, made his way to Woodrow High House and his lady love, Lady Helena Stanhope. She hid him from his enemies in the Grotto, a small, secluded building some 250 yards from the house. It has a domed octagon and is decorated with patterns of black and white pebbles.

One night, as she took supper to him through the moonlit

garden, under the trees and down the path to the Grotto, she was observed by his pursuers. They waited for her to return to the house and then entered the Grotto and killed Sir Peter. The next time Lady Helena went to her lover, she found him dead. She had unwittingly betrayed his hiding place. In great distress, weeping and wringing her hands, she ran back to the house and into the Cromwell Room, where she took poison and died in anguish.

Now it is said the sound of her swishing skirts is heard as her ghost roams the house and makes the trip down to the Grotto, only to return weeping for her lost love to the room where she died. There is a picture of her in one of the rooms of the house, looking beautiful in her green dress, and every so often The Green Lady Ball is held at which she is confidently expected to appear.

Index